Frank Taussig

The Tariff History
of the
United States

Elibron Classics
www.elibron.com

Elibron Classics series.

© 2005 Adamant Media Corporation.

ISBN 1-4021-9785-3 (paperback)
ISBN 1-4021-1667-5 (hardcover)

This Elibron Classics Replica Edition is an unabridged facsimile
of the edition published in 1888 by G. P. Putnam's Sons,
New York and London.

THE TARIFF HISTORY

OF THE

UNITED STATES

A SERIES OF ESSAYS

BY

F. W. TAUSSIG, LL.B., Ph.D.

ASSISTANT PROFESSOR OF POLITICAL ECONOMY IN HARVARD UNIVERSITY

———

NEW YORK & LONDON

G. P. PUTNAM'S SONS

The Knickerbocker Press

1888

Press of

G. P. PUTNAM'S SONS

New York

PREFATORY NOTE.

Of the papers printed in this volume none is now presented to the public for the first time. The essay on " Protection to Young Industries, as Applied in the United States " was first published in Cambridge in 1882, and was republished in a revised edition in New York in 1883. The paper on the tariff of 1828 appeared in the *Political Science Quarterly* for March, 1888. That on the history of the tariff between 1830 and 1860, was printed in the *Quarterly Journal of Economics* for April, 1888. The " History of the Present Tariff " was published in New York in 1885. All, however, have been revised for the present volume, and considerable additions have been made. Repetitions have been avoided, so far as this was possible, and I have attempted to connect the narrative of the separate parts. Although not originally written with the design of presenting a complete history of our tariff legislation, these papers cover in some sort the entire period from 1789 to 1887.

F. W. TAUSSIG.

CAMBRIDGE, Mass, July, 1888.

CONTENTS.

PROTECTION TO YOUNG INDUSTRIES AS APPLIED IN THE UNITED STATES.

I.

THE ARGUMENT FOR PROTECTION TO YOUNG INDUSTRIES.

OF the arguments in favor of protection, none has been more frequently or more sincerely urged than that which is expressed in the phrase " protection to young industries." None has received so generally the approval of economists, even of those little disposed to acknowledge the validity of any reasoning not in accordance with the theory of free exchange. Mill gave it the weight of his approval in a passage which has been frequently cited. Later English writers have followed him in granting its intrinsic soundness. The reasoning of List, the most prominent protectionist writer among the Germans, is based, so far as it is purely economic, on this argument, and since List's time the argument has taken an established place in German treatises on political economy, even though it be admitted that the conditions to which it fairly applies belong to the past.

The argument is, in brief, that it may be advantageous to encourage by legislation a branch of industry which might be profitably carried on, which is therefore sure to be carried on eventually, but whose rise is prevented for the time being by artificial or accidental causes. The essential point of the argument lies in the assumption that the causes which prevent the rise of the industry, and render protection necessary, are not natural and permanent causes,—not such as would permanently prevent, under a state of freedom, the growth of the industry. Let it be supposed, for instance, that the industry to be encouraged is the cotton manufacture. The natural advantages of a given country for making cotton cloths are good, we may suppose, in comparison with the advantages for producing other things. The raw material is cheap, power for machinery is abundant, the general intelligence and industry of the people—which, since they admit of but very slow change, must be considered natural advantages—are such as to fit them for complex industrial operations. There is no permanent cause why cotton goods should not be obtained at as low cost by making them at home as by importing them ; perhaps they can even be produced at lower cost at home. But the cotton manufacture, let it be further supposed, is new ; the machinery used is unknown and complicated, and requires skill and experience of a kind not attainable in other branches of production. The industry of the country runs by custom in other grooves, from which it is not easily diverted. If, at the same time, the communication of knowledge be slow, and enterprise be hesitating, we have a set of conditions under which the establishment of the cotton manufacture may be prevented, long after it might have been carried on with advantage. Under such circumstances it may be wise to encourage the manufacture by duties on imported goods, or by other analogous measures. Sooner or later the cotton manufacture will be introduced and carried on, even without assistance; and the government's aid will only cause it to be established with less friction, and at an earlier date, than would otherwise have been the case.

It may illustrate more clearly the conditions under which such assistance may be useful, to point out those under which it is superfluous. The mere fact that an industry is young in years—has been undertaken only within a short period of time—does not supply the conditions under which protection is justified by this argument. An industry recently established, but similar in kind to other branches of production already carried on in the country, would hardly come within its scope. But where the industry is not only new, but forms a departure from the usual track of production; where, perhaps, machinery of an entirely strange character, or processes hitherto unknown, are necessary; where the skill and experience required are such as could not be attained in the occupations already in vogue; under these circumstances protection may be applied with good results, if no natural disadvantages, in addition to the artificial obstacles, stand in the way. The manufacture of linen goods in the United States, at the present time, probably supplies an example of an industry which, though comparatively new, can hardly be said to deserve protection as a young industry. The methods and machinery in use are not essentially different from those of other branches of textile manufactures. No great departure from the usual track of production is necessary in order to make linens. Manufacturers of the same general character are established on all sides. Work-people and managers with experience in similar work can be easily found. Moreover, the means of obtaining and communicating knowledge at the present time are such that information in regard to the methods and machinery of other countries can be easily obtained, while workmen can be brought from abroad without difficulty. Those artificial obstacles which might temporarily prevent the rise of the industry do not exist, and it may be inferred that, if there are no permanent causes which prevent linens from being made as cheaply in the United States as in other countries, the manufacture will be undertaken and carried on without needing any stimulus from protecting duties.

There are two sets of conditions under which it is supposable that advantages not natural or inherent may be found in one country as compared with another, under which causes merely temporary and accidental may prevent the rise of certain branches of industry in the second country, and under which, therefore, there may be room for the application of protection. These are, first, the state of things in a new country which is rapidly growing in population, and in which, as population becomes more dense, there is a natural change from exclusive devotion to the extractive industries toward greater attention to those branches of production classed as manufactures. The transition from a purely agricultural state to a more diversified system of industry may be retarded, in the complete absence of other occupations than agriculture, beyond the time when it might advantageously take place. Secondly, when great improvements take place in some of the arts of production, it is possible that the new process may be retained in the country in which they originate, and may fail to be applied in another country, through ignorance, the inertia of habit, and perhaps in consequence of restrictive legislation at the seat of the new methods. Here, again, the obstacles to the intro- duction of the new industry may be of that artificial kind which can be overcome most easily by artificial means. Now, both these sets of conditions seem to have been ful- filled in the United States in the beginning of the present century. The country was normally emerging, to a con- siderable extent, from that state of almost exclusive devo- tion to agriculture which had characterized the colonies. At the same time great changes were taking place in the mechanical arts, and new processes, hardly known outside of England, and held under a practical monopoly there, were revolutionizing the methods of manufacturing production. Under these circumstances there would seem to have existed room for the legitimate application of protection for young industries.

The more detailed examination in the following pages of the industrial condition of the country during the earlier part of this century will bring out more clearly the reasons why protection may then have been useful. It may be well, however, to notice at this point one difference between those days and the present which must seriously affect the application of the argument we are considering. Even if we were to suppose the conditions of 1810 to exist now; if the country were now first beginning to attempt manufactures, and if a great revolution in manufacturing industry happened to make the attempt peculiarly difficult; even then the obstacles arising from the force of custom, and from the want of familiarity with new processes, would be much more easy to overcome now than sixty years ago. The ties of custom in industry have become much loosened in the last half century; capital and labor turn more easily to new employments. The railroad, the telegraph, the printing-press, the immense increase in the facility of communication, the constant change in methods of production in all industries, have tended to make new discoveries and inventions common property, and to do away with advantages in production based on other than permanent causes. It is true that there are still appreciable differences in the arts of production in different countries, and that some may have a superiority over others based on the merely accidental or temporary possession of better processes or more effective machinery. But the United States hardly lag behind in the industrial advance of the present day, and where they do labor under artificial or factitious disadvantages, these cannot endure long or be of great consequence under a system of freedom.

Sixty years ago, however, the state of things was very different. The conditions were then in force under which protection might be needed to enable useful industries to be carried on. The argument for protection to young industries was accordingly the most effective of those urged in favor of the protective policy. During the twenty years which followed the war of 1812 the protective controversy was one of the most important features in the political life of the nation; and the young industries argument was the great rallying-cry of the protectionists. It is of interest to examine how far protection of the kind advocated was actually applied, and how far it was the cause, or an essential condition, of that rise of manufactures which took place. The object of this paper is to make such an investigation.

II.

THE INDUSTRIAL HISTORY OF THE UNITED STATES, AND THE COURSE OF PROTECTIVE LEGISLATION, FROM 1789 TO 1838.

THE early economic history of the United States may be divided into two periods. The first, which is in the main a continuation of the colonial period, lasted till about the year 1808 ; the embargo marks the beginning of the series of events which closed it. The second began in 1808, and lasted through the generation following. It was during the second period that the most decided attempt was made to apply protection to young industries in the United States, and with this period we are chiefly concerned.

During the first period the country was, on the whole, in the same industrial condition in which the colonies had been. The colonies had been necessarily engaged almost exclusively in agriculture, and in the occupations closely connected with it. The agricultural community could not get on without blacksmiths, carpenters, masons, shoemakers, and other artisans, and these existed side by side with the farmers. In those days, it must be remembered, handicraft workmen of this kind occupied a more import-ant place in industrial organizations than they do at the present time. They made many articles and performed many services which are now the objects of manufacturing production and of extensive trade, and come within the range of international dealings. Many tools were then made by individual blacksmiths, many wares by the car-penter, many homespun cloths fulled and finished at the small fulling-mill. Production of this kind necessarily takes place at the locality where consumption goes on. In those days the division of labor between distant bodies of men had been carried out to a comparatively slight extent, and the scope of international trade was therefore much more limited. The existence of these handicraft workmen accounts for the numerous notices of " manu-factures " which Mr. Bishop industriously collected in his " History of Manufactures," and is not inconsistent with the mainly extractive character of the industry of the colonies. What could be imported at that time was im-ported, and was paid for by the exportation of agricul-tural produce. The exportation took place, so far as the northern colonies were concerned, largely to the West Indies. From the West India trade the means for pay-ing indirectly for the imported goods were mainly ob-tained. There were some important exceptions to this general state of things. Ship-building was carried on to a considerable extent in New England, where abundance of material and the necessity of transportation by water

made such an industry natural.   The production of unmanufactured iron was carried on to a considerable extent ;
for at that time the production of pig and bar iron tended
to fix itself in those countries where wood, the fuel then
used, was abundant, and was therefore an industry much
more analogous to agriculture than it has been since the
employment of coal as fuel.   In the main, however, the
colonies made only such manufactures as could not be imported.   All manufactured goods that could be imported
were not made at home, but obtained in exchange for
agricultural exports.

This state of things was little changed after the end of
the Revolutionary war and the adoption of the Constitution.   The year 1789 marks no such epoch in economic as it
does in political history.   Agriculture, commerce, and the
necessary mechanic arts, continued to form the main occupations of the people.   Such goods as could be imported
continued to be obtained from abroad in exchange for
exports, mainly of agricultural produce.   The range of
importable articles was, it is true, gradually extending.
Cloths, linens, and textile fabrics were still chiefly homespun, and fine goods of this kind were still in the main
the only textile fabrics imported.   But with the great
growth of manufacturing industry in England during this
time, the range of articles that could be imported was
growing wider and wider.   During the Napoleonic wars the
American market was much the most important for the
newly established English manufactures.   Large quanti-

ties of cotton and woollen goods were imported, and the importations of manufactures of iron, in regard to which a similar change in production was then taking place, also increased steadily. Sooner or later the change in the course of production which was going on in England must have had, and did have, a strong influence on the economic condition of the United States; but for the time being this influence was little felt, and the country continued in the main to run in the grooves of the colonial period.

This absence of development was strongly promoted by the peculiar condition of the foreign trade of the country up to 1808. The wars of the French Revolution opened to this country profitable markets for its agricultural products in the West Indies and in Europe, and profitable employment for its shipping, both in carrying the increased exports and in a more or less authorized trade between the belligerent countries and their colonies. For many years the gains arising from these sources, though not regular or undisturbed, were great, and afforded every inducement to remain in the occupations that yielded them. The demand for agricultural products for exportation to the belligerent countries and their colonies was large, and the prices of wheat, corn, and meat were correspondingly high. The heavy exports and the profits on freights furnished abundant means for paying for imported goods. Importations were therefore large, and imported goods were so cheap as to afford little inducement for engaging in the production of similar goods at home.[1]

The tariff legislation of this period was naturally much influenced by the direction taken by the industries of the

[1] The following tables of imports and exports show the influence of these circumstances on the foreign trade of the country. The exports of foreign produce show the swelling of the carrying-trade. The price of flour shows the effect on the prices of agricultural produce. The influence of the temporary stoppage of the war in Europe during the time of the Peace of Amiens is clearly seen.

Year.	Gross Imports. 000 Omitted.	Gross Exports 000 Omitted.	Exports of Foreign Produce. 000 Omitted	Price of Flour per Bbl.
1791	29,200	19,000	500	. . .
92	31,500	20,700	1,750	$ 5.07
93	31 100	26,100	2,100	6.21
94	34,600	33,000	6,500	7.22
95	69,750	48,000	8,500	12.05
96	81,400	67,000	26,300	12.43
97	75,400	56,800	27,000	9 00
98	68,500	61,500	33,000	8.78
99	79,000	78,600	45,500	9.62
1800	91,200	71,000	39,100	9.85
01	111,300	94,000	46,600	10.45
Peace of 02	76,300	72,000	35,700	6.75 ⎫
Amiens. 03	64,700	55,800	13,600	6.73 ⎭
04	85,000	77,700	36,200	8.22
05	120,600	95,500	53,200	10.28
06	129,400	101,500	60,300	7 30
07	138,500	108,300	59,600	7.00
08	57,000	22,400	13,000	5.60
09	59,400	52,200	20,800	6.90
10	85,400	66,700	24,400	9.66
11	53,400	61,300	16,000	0.00
12	77,000	38,500	8,500	8.75
13	22,000	27,900	2,800	8 50
14	13,000	6,900	150	7.70

The tables of imports and exports are from the Treasury Reports. The last table, giving the price of flour, is in "American State Papers, Finance," III., 536.

country. The peculiarly favorable conditions under which agriculture and commerce were carried on prevented the growth of any strong feeling in favor of assisting manufactures. Much has been said in the course of the protective controversy about the views of the fathers of the republic. But for nearly twenty years after the formation of the Union other subjects so absorbed the attention of public men that no distinct opinion appears in their utterances for or against protective duties. Considering the state of economic knowledge in those days, the example set by European countries, and the application of the colonial system before the days of independence, we cannot be surprised that some disposition was shown to impose protective duties. It is curious that in the first session of Congress these were advocated most earnestly by the representatives from Pennsylvania, who took their stand from the first as unflinching advocates of a protective policy. On the other hand, the current toward more liberal views, which had set in so strongly after the writings of the French economists and the publication of the "Wealth of Nations," had made its way to the United States. One might expect to find its influence most strong among the followers of Jefferson, whose political philosophy led them in general to oppose government interference. But both Federalists and Republicans were influenced in their attitude to the question of protection most of all by its bearing on the other more prominent questions on which parties began to be divided.

Madison had maintained the principle of free intercourse in 1789,[1] and Jefferson in 1787 had extolled the virtues of a simple agricultural State.[2] But in 1793, when the Federalists and Republicans began to differ on questions of foreign policy, and especially on the attitude the country should take in the wars of the French Revolution, Jefferson advocated vigorous measures of protection directed against England, and Madison brought forward a set of resolutions based on his recommendations.[3] On the other hand, Fisher Ames had said, in 1789, that the general government should nurture those industries in which the individual States had an interest ; but in 1794, when his political views led him to oppose Madison's resolutions, he called the whole theory of protection an exploded dogma.[4] It has often been said that the first tariff act, that of 1789, was a protective measure, and that in the debate on it the protective controversy appeared fullgrown. But such considerations had little to do with the act ; and the discussions on protection by no means indicate what was the real centre of interest.[5] The act was modelled on the five per cent. import duty, which the

[1] "Annals of Congress," 1789, pp. 112–114.

[2] "Notes on Virginia, Works," VIII., 404.

[3] See Jefferson's "Report on Commerce, Works," VII., 637 ; and Madison's resolutions of 1794, based on Jefferson's Report, "Annals of Congress," 1794, pp. 155, 209.

[4] "Annals of Congress," 1789, p. 221 ; 1794, p. 342.

[5] It is significant, for example, that Madison's letters to Jefferson, then in Paris, about the debates on the tariff act of 1789, make no reference whatever to the protective discussion. Madison's "Works," I., 466, 480.

Congress of the Confederation had tried in vain to impose, and its main object was to secure revenue for the new government, whose successful working was the one end which all the legislation of the first few years sought to bring about. The general level of duties was five per cent. on the value. On certain articles of luxury, higher ad valorem rates were fixed, the highest being fifteen per cent. on carriages. In certain specific duties, on articles like hemp, cordage, nails, iron manufactures, and glass, there was doubtless an intention of aiding the domestic producers.[1] Some of these articles were selected because it was supposed they would be needed in time of war. On others it is not unlikely that a concession to protective demands was made by those who had at heart the success of the new government, in order to insure the passage of the indispensable revenue act.[2]

The same general state of feeling and the same policy continued during the twenty years following. For a short time after 1789, it may be possible to detect a drift in favor of protective duties,[3] which doubtless was strength-

---

[1] It seems to have been understood that the duties on these articles were made specific with this intention. See a brief report by Hamilton in his "Works," II., 55.

[2] This suggestion is made in Professor H. C. Adams's essay on "Taxation in the United States," 1789–1816, in the "Johns Hopkins University Studies," vol. II., pp. 29, 30. The reader who wishes further information is referred to this excellent monograph.

[3] A number of committee reports on petitions for higher duties are printed in "American State Papers, Finance," vols. I., II. After 1794 the reports are generally against the petitions.

ened by the powerful advocacy of protection in Hamilton's " Report on Manufactures " (1792). But that famous document had little, if any, effect on legislation. The moderate policy of 1789 was maintained. The duties were increased from time to time as more revenue was needed, but they were in all cases moderate. Those which were most distinctly protective aimed to assist industries which already had a good foothold, and they had no appreciable influence in diverting the industry of the country into new channels. No action at all was taken for the encouragement of the production of textiles, of crude iron, and of the other articles which later became the great subjects of dispute in the protective controversy.

The industrial situation changed abruptly in 1808. The complications with England and France led to a series of measures which mark a turning-point in the industrial history of the country. The Berlin and Milan decrees of Napoleon, and the English orders in Council, led, in December, 1807, to the Embargo. The Non-Intercourse Act followed in 1809. War with England was declared in 1812. During the war, intercourse with England was prohibited, and all import duties were doubled. The last-mentioned measure was adopted in the hope of increasing the revenue, but had little effect, for foreign trade practically ceased to exist. This series of restrictive measures blocked the accustomed channels of exchange and production, and gave an enormous stimulus to those branches of industry whose products had before been imported. Establishments for the manufacture of cotton goods, woollen cloths, iron, glass, pottery, and other articles, sprang up with a mushroom growth. We shall have occasion to refer more in detail to this growth when the history of some of these manufactures comes to be considered separately. It is sufficient here to note that the restrictive legislation of 1808-15 was, for the time being, equivalent to extreme protection. The consequent rise of a considerable class of manufacturers, whose success depended largely on the continuance of protection, formed the basis of a strong movement for more decided limitation of foreign competition.

Some signs of the gradual growth of a protective feeling appear before the close of the war.[1] It was natural that the patriotic fervor which the events of the period of restriction and war called out for the first time in our history, should bring with it a disposition to encourage the production at home of a number of manufactured articles, of which the sudden interruption in the foreign supply caused great inconvenience. Madison, whose views on this subject, as on others, shifted as time went on and circumstances changed, recommended the encouragement of manufactures ; and in some of Clay's earlier speeches we can see the first signs of the American system of the

---

[1] It is curious to note that in 1802–1804, during the temporary lull that followed the Peace of Amiens, the committee reports seem to show a drift toward protection. See " American State Papers, Finance," II., pp. 29, 80, and the report on the Barbary Powers Act of 1804, " Annals of Congress," 1804, pp. 946–950.

future.[1] The feeling in favor of the manufactures that had sprung up during the time of restriction obtained some clear concessions in the tariff act of 1816. The control of the policy of Congress at that time was in the hands of a knot of young men of the rising generation, who had brought about the war and felt in a measure responsible for its results. There was a strong feeling among these that the manufacturing establishments which had grown up during the war should be assisted. There was little feeling, however, either in Congress or among the people, such as appeared in later years, in favor of a permanent strong protective policy. Higher duties were therefore granted on those goods in whose production most interest was felt, textile fabrics ; but only for a limited period. Cotton and woollen goods were to pay 25 per cent. till 1819 ; after that date they were to pay 20 per cent. A proviso, intended to make more secure this measure of protection, was adopted in regard to a minimum duty on cotton goods, to which reference will be made in another connection. These and some other distinctly protective provisions were defended by Calhoun, mainly on the ground of the need of making provision for the exigencies of another war ; and on that ground they were adopted, and at the same time limited. The general increase of

---

[1] See Madison's message of 1809, "Statesman's Manual," I., 289 ; and Clay's speech of 1810, "Works," I., 195. Madison never gave up his general acceptance of the principle of free trade, but admitted it to be inapplicable to articles needed in time of war, and in circumstances to which the young-industries' argument applied. See his " Works," III., 42.

duties under the act of 1816, to an average of about twenty per cent., was due to the necessity of providing for the payment of the interest on the heavy debt contracted during the war.

For some time after the close of the war and the enactment of the tariff of 1816, there was no pressure for a more vigorous application of protective principles. The general expectation was, that the country would fall back into much the same state of things as that which had existed before 1808 ; that agriculture and commerce would again be as profitable as during the previous period, and would be as exclusively the occupations of the people. Such an expectation could not in the nature of things be entirely fulfilled, but for a time it was encouraged by several accidental circumstances. The harvests in Europe for several seasons were bad, and caused a stronger demand and higher price for the staple food products. The demand for cotton was large, and the price high. Most important of all, the currency was in a state of complete disarrangement, and concealed and supported an unsound economic condition. Under cover of the excessive issues of practically irredeemable bank-notes, the prices of all commodities were high, as were the general rates of wages and rents. The prices of bread-stuffs and provisions, the staples of the North, and of cotton and tobacco, the staples of the South, were high, not only absolutely, but relatively, and encouraged continued large production of these articles. The prices of most manufactured goods were comparatively low.   After the war the imports of these from England were very heavy.   The long pent-up stream of English merchandise may be said to have flooded the world at the close of the Napoleonic wars. In this country, as in others, imports were carried beyond the capacity for consumption, and prices fell much below the normal rates.   The strain of this over-supply and fall of prices bore hard on the domestic manufacturers, especially on those who had begun and carried on operations during the restrictive period ; and many of them were compelled to cease production and to abandon their works.

This abnormal period, which had its counterpart of feverish excitement and speculation in Europe, came to an end in 1818–19.   The civilized world then settled down to recover slowly from the effects of a generation of war and destruction.   In the United States the currency bubble was pricked in the latter part of 1818. Prices began to fall rapidly and heavily, and continued to fall through 1819.   The prices of the agricultural staples of the North and South underwent the greatest change, for the harvests in Europe were again good in 1818, the English corn-laws of 1816 went into operation, and the demand for cotton fell off.   A new scale of monetary exchange gradually went into operation.   During the period of transition there was, as there always is in such periods, much suffering and uneasiness ; but gradually the difficulties of adjusting old contracts and engagements were overcome, and the habits of the people accommodated themselves to the new régime. Within three or four years after 1819 the effects of the crash were no longer felt in most parts of the country.

Two results which it is important to note in this connection followed from the crisis of 1819: first, a great alteration in the position and prospects of manufacturing industries; and second, the rise of a strong public feeling in favor of protecting these industries, and the final enactment of legislation for that purpose. The first of these results was due primarily to the fact that the fall in prices after 1819 did not so greatly affect most manufactured goods as it did other articles. The prices of manufactured goods had already declined, in consequence of the heavy importations in the years immediately following the war. When, therefore, the heavy fall took place in 1819 in the prices of food and of raw materials, in the gains of agriculture, in money wages and money rents, the general result was advantageous for the manufacturers. They were put into a position to produce with profit at the lower prices which had before been unprofitable, and to meet more easily foreign competition. After the first shock was over, and the system of exchange became cleared of the confusion and temporary stoppage which must attend all great fluctuations in prices, this result was plainly felt.[1] It is easy to see that the whole process

---

[1] " The abundance of capital, indicated by the avidity with which loans are taken at the reduced rate of five per cent., the reduction in the wages of labor, and the decline in the price of property of all kinds, all concur favorably for domestic manufactures."—Clay, Speech of 1820. " Works," I., 419.

was nothing more than the evolution of the new state of things which was to take the place of that of the period before 1808. In that earlier period manufactured goods, so far as they could be obtained by importation at all, were imported cheaply and easily by means of large exports and freight earnings. These resources were now largely cut o... Exports declined, and imports in the end had to follow them. The tightening of the English corn-law, and the general restriction of trade and navigation by England and other countries, contributed to strengthen this tendency, and necessarily served to stimulate the growth of manufactures in the United States. That growth was indeed complicated and made more striking by the revolution which was then taking place in many departments of manufacturing industry. Especially in the production of textile fabrics, machinery was rapidly displacing—in England had already largely displaced—production by hand on a small scale. Home-spun textiles were gradually making room for the products of the spinning-jenny and the power-loom. The state of things that followed the crisis of 1818–19 was favorable to the rise of manufactures; but the change took place not so much by an increase in the relative number of persons engaged in such occupations, as in the substitution of manufactures in the modern sense for the more simple methods of the previous period.[1]

---

[1] According to the census returns of 1820 and 1840, the only two of the earlier returns in which occupations are enumerated, there were engaged

The second effect of the change that followed the financial crisis of 1819, was the strong protective movement which exercised so important an influence on the political history of the next generation. The diminution of the foreign demand, and the fall in the prices of staple products, naturally gave rise to a cry for a home market. The absence of reciprocity and the restrictive regulations of England, especially in face of the comparatively liberal import duties of this country, furnished an effective argument to the advocates of protection. Most effective, however, was the argument for protection to young industries, which was urged with persistency during the next ten or

---

in manufactures and the mechanic arts in 1820, 13.7 per cent. of the working population ; in 1840, 17.1 per cent. In New England 21 per cent. were so engaged in 1820, 30.2 per cent. in 1840 ; in the Middle States 22.6 per cent. in 1820, 28 per cent. in 1840. Mac Gregor, "Progress of America," II., 101. There are no census figures before 1820. In 1807 it was loosely estimated that out of 2,358,000 persons actively employed, 230,000 were engaged in mechanics and manufactures—less than 10 per cent. Blodgett, "Thoughts on a Plan of Economy," etc. [1807] p. 6.

The fluctuations in the exports of wheat flour, which was the most important article of export among agricultural products during the early part of the century, tell plainly the story of the country's foreign trade. They were as follows, the figures indicating millions of dollars :

Yearly average,	1803–7 (expanded trade)	8.2
" "	1808–10 (restriction)	4.0
" "	1810–12 (restrictions removed) . .	13.5
" "	1813–15 (war)	5.5
" "	1816–17 (temporary revival) . .	14.5
Year 1818	. . . . . .	6.0
" 1819	. . . . . .	5.0
" 1820	. . . . . .	4.3

During the decade 1820–1830, when matters settled down to a normal state, the yearly export was between four and five millions of dollars. See "Quarterly Reports of the Bureau of Statistics," 1883–84, No. 4, pp. 523, 524.

fifteen years. The character and history of this early protective movement will be discussed elsewhere.[1] Here it is
sufficient to note that its effect on legislation was not
merely to maintain the protective provisions of the tariff
of 1816, but much to extend the protective element in
tariff legislation. Already in 1818 it had been enacted
that the duty of 25 per cent. on cottons and woollens
should remain in force till 1826, instead of being reduced
to 20 per cent. in 1819, as had been provided by the act of
1816. At the same time the duty on all forms of unmanufactured iron was considerably raised ; a measure to
which we shall have occasion to refer in another connection. In 1820, while the first pressure of the economic
revulsion bore hard on the people, a vigorous attempt
was made to pass a high protective tariff, and it barely
failed of success, by a single vote in the Senate. In 1824
the protectionists succeeded in passing the tariff of that
year, which increased all duties considerably. Four years
later, in the tariff of 1828, the protective movement
reached its highest point. The measures which followed
in 1832 and 1833 moderated the peculiarly offensive provisions of the act of 1828, but retained the essential parts
of protection for some years longer. On the whole, from
1816 on, there was applied for some twenty years a continuous policy of protection ; for the first eight years with
much moderation, but after 1824 with high duties, and
stringent measures for enforcing them.

---

[1] In the next essay, pp. 68–75.

III.

THE COTTON MANUFACTURE.

WE turn now to the history of some of the industries to which protection was applied during this long period, in order to determine, so far as this is possible, how far their introduction and early growth were promoted or rendered possible by protection. We shall try to see how far and with what success protection to young industries was applied. The most important of them, on account both of its magnitude and of the peculiarly direct application of protection to it, is the cotton manufacture; and we are fortunate in having, at the same time, the fullest and most trustworthy accounts of the early history of this industry.[1]

During the first of the two periods into which we have divided the early economic history of the United States, several attempts were made to introduce the manufacture of cotton by the machinery invented by Hargreaves and Arkwright in the latter part of the 18th century. One or

---

[1] In S. Batchelder's "Introduction and Early Progress of the Cotton Manufacture in the U. S." (1863); G. S. White's "Memoir of Samuel Slater" (1836); and N. Appleton's "Introduction of the Power-loom and Origin of Lowell" (1858).

two of these attempts succeeded, but most of them failed, and the manufacture, which then was growing with marvellous rapidity in England, failed to attain any considerable development in this country.   In 1787 a factory using the new machinery was established at Beverly, Mass., and obtained aid from the State treasury; but it was soon abandoned.   Similar unsuccessful ventures were made at Bridgewater, Mass., Norwich, Conn., and Pawtucket, R. I., as well as in Philadelphia.   The spinning-jenny was introduced in all these, but never successfully operated.[1] The first successful attempt to manufacture with the new machinery was made by Samuel Slater, at Pawtucket, R. I.   Slater was a workman who had been employed in Arkwright's factories in England.   He joined to mechanical skill strong business capacity.   He had become familiar with the system of carding, drawing, roving, and mule-spinning.   Induced to come to the United States in 1798 by prizes offered by the Philadelphia Society for Promoting Manufactures, he took charge in the following year of a cotton-factory which had been begun and carried on with little success by some Quakers of Pawtucket.   He was successful in setting up the Arkwright machinery, and became the founder of the cotton manufacture in this country. Through him machinery, and instruction in using it, were obtainable; and a few other factories were begun under

---

[1] Batchelder, p. 26 *seq.;* White, ch. III.   The cotton-mill at Norwich, built in 1790, was operated for ten years, and then abandoned as unprofitable.—Caulkins, " Hist. of Norwich," p. 696.

his superintendence.   Nevertheless, the manufacture
hardly maintained its hold.   In 1803 there were only four
factories in the country.[1]   The cotton manufacture was at
that time extending in England at a rapid rate, and the
imports of cotton goods from England were large.   The
Treasury reports of those days give no separate statements
of the imports of cotton goods; but in 1807 it was estimated that the imports of cotton goods from England
amounted to eleven million dollars' worth—a very large
sum for those days.[2]   The consumption of cotton goods
was large; but only an insignificant part of it was supplied
by home production, although later developments showed
that this branch of industry could be carried on with distinct success.   The ease with which these imports were
paid for, and the stimulus which this period, as described
in the preceding pages, gave to agriculture and commerce, account in part for the slowness with which the
domestic manufacture developed.   The fact that raw cotton was not yet grown to any considerable extent in the
country, together, doubtless, with the better machinery
and larger experience and skill of the English, account for
the rest.

When, however, the period of restriction began, in
1808, the importation of foreign goods was first impeded,
and soon entirely prevented.   The domestic manufacture
accordingly extended with prodigious rapidity.   Already

---

[1] Bishop, " Hist. of Manufactures," II., 102.
[2] See the pamphlet by Blodgett " On a Plan of Economy," etc., already
cited, p. 26.

during the years 1804–8 greater activity must have prevailed ; for in the latter year fifteen mills had been built running 8,000 spindles. In 1809 the number of mills built shot up to 62, with 31,000 spindles, and while 25 more mills were in course of erection.[1] In 1812 there were 50 factories within thirty miles of Providence, operating nearly 60,000 spindles, and capable of operating 100,000.[2] During the war the same rapid growth continued, rendered possible as it was by the increasing supply of raw cotton from the South. The number of spindles was said to be 80,000 in 1811, and 500,000 in 1815. In 1800, 500 bales of cotton had been used ; in 1805, 1,000 bales. In 1810 the number consumed rose to 10,000 ; in 1815, it was 90,000.[3] These figures cannot be supposed to be

---

[1] Gallatin's Report on Manufactures in 1810 ; " Amer. State Papers, Finance," II., 427.

[2] " White : " Memoir of Slater," p. 188.

[3] See the Report of a Committee of Congress on the Cotton Manufacture in 1816 ; " Amer. State Papers, Finance," III, 82, 84. This estimate refers only to the cotton consumed in factories, and does not include that used in household manufacture. The number of spindles for 1815, as given in this report, is probably much too large. In Woodbury's Report of 1836 on cotton, the number of spindles in use in factories is given as follows :

In 1805	.	.	4,500 spindles.
" 1807	.	.	8,000 "
" 1809	.	.	31,000 "
" 1810	.	.	87,000 "
" 1815	.	.	130,000 "
" 1820	.	.	220,000 "
" 1821	.	.	230,000 "
" 1825	.	.	800,000 "

" Exec. Doc.," 1 Sess., 24 Congr , No. 146. p. 51. It need not be said that these figures are hopelessly loose ; but they are sufficient to support the general assertions of the text.

at all accurate; but they indicate clearly an enormously rapid development of the manufacture of cotton.

The machinery in almost all these new factories was for spinning yarn only. Weaving was still carried on by the hand-loom, usually by weavers working in considerable numbers on account for manufacturers. Toward the end of the war, however, a change began to be made almost as important in the history of textile manufactures as the use of the spinning-jenny and mule: namely, the substitution of the power-loom for the hand-loom. The introduction of the power-loom took place in England at about the same time, and some intimation of its use seems to have reached the inventor in this country, Francis C. Lowell. He perfected the machine, however, without any use of English models, in the course of the year 1814. In the same year it was put in operation at a factory at Waltham, Mass. There for the first time the entire process of converting cotton into cloth took place under one roof. The last important step in giving textile manufactures their present form was thus taken.[1]

When peace was made in 1815, and imports began again, the newly established factories, most of which were badly equipped and loosely managed, met with serious embarrassment. Many were entirely abandoned. The manufacturers petitioned Congress for assistance; and they received, in 1816, that measure of help which the public was then disposed to grant. The tariff of 1816

[1] Appleton, pp. 7-11; Batchelder, pp. 60-70.

levied a duty of 25 per cent. on cotton goods for three years, a duty considered sufficiently protective in those days of inexperience in protective legislation. At the same time it was provided that all cotton cloths, costing less than 25 cents a yard, should be considered to have cost 25 cents and be charged with duty accordingly; that is, should be charged 25 per cent. of 25 cents, or 6¼ cents a yard, whatever their real value or cost. This was the first of the minimum valuation provisos which played so considerable a part in later tariff legislation, and which have been maintained in large part to the present time. A similar minimum duty was imposed on cotton-yarns.[1] At the time when these measures were passed, the minimum provisos hardly served to increase appreciably the weight of the duty of 25 per cent. Coarse cotton cloths were then worth from 25 to 30 cents, and, even without the provisos, would have paid little, if any thing, less than the minimum duty. But, after 1818, the use of the power-loom, and the fall in the price of raw cotton, combined greatly to reduce the prices of cotton goods. The price of coarse cottons fell to 19 cents in 1819, 13 cents in 1826, and 8½ cents in 1829.[2] The minimum duty became proportionately heavier as the price decreased, and, in a few years after its enactment, had become prohibitive of the importation of the coarser kinds of cotton cloths.

---

[1] The minimum system seems to have been suggested by Lowell.   Appleton, p. 13. Compare Appleton's speech in Congress in 1833.—"Congressional Debates," IX., 1213.

[2] Appleton, p. 16.

During the years immediately after the war, the aid given in the tariff of 1816 was not sufficient to prevent severe depression in the cotton manufacture. Reference has already been made to the disadvantages which, under the circumstances of the years 1815–18, existed for all manufacturers who had to meet competition from abroad. But when the crisis of 1818–19 had brought about a re-arrangement of prices more advantageous for manufacturers, matters began to mend. The minimum duty became more effective in handicapping foreign competitors. At the same time the power-loom was generally introduced. Looms made after an English model were introduced in the factories of Rhode Island, the first going into operation in 1817; while in Massachusetts and New Hampshire the loom invented by Lowell was generally adopted after 1816.[1] From these various causes the manufacture soon became profitable. There is abundant evidence to show that shortly after the crisis the cotton manufacture had fully recovered from the depression that followed the war.[2] The profits made were such as to cause a rapid

---

[1] Appleton, p. 13 ; Batchelder, pp. 70–73.

[2] The following passage, referring to the general revival of manufactures, may be quoted : " The manufacture of cotton now yields a moderate profit to those who conduct the business with the requisite skill and economy. The extensive factories at Pawtucket are still in operation. . . . In Philadelphia it is said that about 4,000 looms have been put in operation within the last six months, which are chiefly engaged in making cotton goods, and that in all probability they will, within six months more, be increased to four times that number. In Paterson, N. J., where, two years ago, only three out of sixteen of its extensive factories were in operation . . . all are now in vigorous employment."—" Niles's Register," XXI., 39 (1821). Com-

extension of the industry. The beginning of those manufacturing villages which now form the characteristic
economic feature of New England falls in this period.
Nashua was founded in 1823. Fall River, which had
grown into some importance during the war of 1814, grew
rapidly from 1820 to 1830.[1] By far the most important
and the best known of the new ventures in cotton manufacturing was the foundation of the town of Lowell, which
was undertaken by the same persons who had been engaged in the establishment of the first power-loom factory
at Waltham. The new town was named after the inventor
of the power-loom. The scheme of utilizing the falls of
the Merrimac, at the point where Lowell now stands, had
been suggested as early as 1821, and in the following year
the Merrimac Manufacturing Company was incorporated.
In 1823 manufacturing began, and was profitable from the
beginning ; and in 1824 the future growth of Lowell was
clearly foreseen.[2]

---

pare *Ibid.*, XXII., 225, 250 (1822) ; XXIII., 35, 88 (1823) ; and *passim.*
In Woodbury's cotton report, cited above, it is said (p. 57) that "there was
a great increase [in cotton manufacturing] in 1806 and 1807 ; again during
the war of 1812 ; again from 1820 to 1825 ; and in 1831–32."

[1] Fox's " History of Dunstable " ; Earl's " History of Fall River," p. 20
seq.

[2] See the account in Appleton, pp. 17–25. One of the originators of the
enterprise said in 1824 : " If our business succeeds, as we have reason to
expect, we shall have here [at Lowell] as large a population in twenty
years from this time as there was in Boston twenty years ago."—Batchelder, p. 69.

In Bishop, II., 309, is a list of the manufacturing villages of 1826, in
which some twenty places are enumerated.

From this sketch of the early history of the cotton manufacture we may draw some conclusions. Before 1808 the difficulties in the way of the introduction of this branch of industry were such that it made little progress. These difficulties were largely artificial; and though the obstacles arising from ignorance of the new processes and from the absence of experienced workmen, were partly removed by the appearance of Slater, they were sufficient, when combined with the stimulus which the condition of foreign trade gave to agriculture and the carrying trade, to prevent any appreciable development. Had this period come to an end without any accompanying political change—had there been no embargo, no non-intercourse act, and no war with England—the growth of the cotton manufacture, however certain to have taken place in the end, might have been subject to much friction and loss. Conjecture as to what might have been is dangerous, especially in economic history, but it seems reasonable to suppose that if the period before 1808 had come to an end without a jar, the eager competition of well-established English manufacturers, the lack of familiarity with the processes, and the long-continued habit, especially in New England, of almost exclusive attention to agriculture, commerce, and the carrying trade, might have rendered slow and difficult the change, however inevitable it may have been, to greater attention to manufactures. Under such circumstances there might have been room for the legitimate application of protection to the cotton manufacture as a young industry. But this period, in fact, came to an end with a violent shock, which threw industry out of its accustomed grooves, and caused the striking growth of the cotton manufacture from 1808 to 1815. The transition caused much suffering, but it took place sharply and quickly. The interruption of trade was equivalent to a rude but vigorous application of protection, which did its work thoroughly. When peace came, in 1815, it found a large number of persons and a great amount of capital engaged in the cotton manufacture, and the new processes of manufacture introduced on an extensive scale. Under such circumstances the industry was certain to be maintained if it was for the economic interest of the country that it should be carried on.

The duties of the tariff of 1816, therefore, can hardly be said to have been necessary. Nevertheless, they may have been of service. The assistance they gave was, it is true, insignificant in comparison with the shelter from all foreign competition during the war. Indeed, most manufacturers desired much higher duties than were granted.[1] It is true, also, that the minimum duty on cottons was least effective during the years immediately after the war, when the price of cottons was higher, and the duty was therefore proportionately less high. But these years be-

---

[1] "In 1816 a new tariff was to be made. The Rhode Island manufacturers were clamorous for a very high specific duty. Mr. Lowell's views on the tariff were much more moderate, and he finally brought Mr. Lowndes and Mr. Calhoun to support the minimum of 6¼ cents a yard, which was carried."—Appleton, p. 13.

tween the close of the war and the general fall of prices in 1819 were trying for the manufacturers. The normal economic state, more favorable for them, was not reached till the crisis of 1818–19 was well over. During the intervening years the minimum duty may have assisted the manufacturers without causing any permanent charge on the people. The fact that careful and self-reliant men, like the founders of the Waltham and Lowell enterprises, were most urgent in advising the adoption of the rates of 1816—at a time, too, when the practice of appealing to Congress for assistance when in distress had not yet become common among manufacturers—may indicate that those rates were of service in encouraging the continuance of the manufacture. How seriously its progress would have been impeded or retarded by the absence of duties, cannot be said. On the whole, although the great impulse to the industry was given during the war, the duties on cottons in the tariff of 1816 may be considered a judicious application of the principle of protection to young industries.

Before 1824, the manufacture, as we have seen, was securely established. The further application of protection in that and in the following years was needless, and, so far as it had any effect, was harmful. The minimum valuation was raised in 1824 to 30 cents, and in 1828 to 35 cents. The minimum duties were thereby raised to $7\frac{1}{2}$ and $8\frac{3}{4}$ cents respectively. By 1824 the manufacture had so firm a hold that its further extension should have been left to individual enterprise, which by that time might have been relied on to carry the industry as far as it was for the economic interest of the country that it should be carried. The increased duties of 1824 and 1828 do not come within the scope of the present discussion.

IV.

THE sudden and striking growth of the cotton manufacture in the last hundred years has caused its history, in this country as in others, to be written with comparative fulness. Of the early history of the manufacture of woollen goods in the United States we have but scanty accounts ; but these are sufficient to show that the general course of events was similar to that in cotton manufacturing. During the colonial period and the years immediately after the Revolution, such woollen cloths as were not spun and woven in households for personal use were imported from England. The goods of household manufacture, however, formed, and for many years after the introduction of machinery continued to form, by far the greater part of those in use. The first attempt at making woollens in large quantities is said to have been made at Ipswich, Mass., in 1792 ; but no machinery seems to have been used in this undertaking. In 1794 the new machinery was for the first time applied to the manufacture of wool, and it is noteworthy that, as in the case of the cotton manufacture, the machinery was introduced by Enlish workmen. These were the brothers Arthur and John Scholfield, who came to the United States in 1793, and in the next year established a factory at Byfield, Mass. Their machinery, however, was exclusively for carding wool, and for dressing (fulling) woollen goods ; and for the latter purpose it was probably in no way different from that of the numerous fulling-mills which were scattered over the country during colonial times. Spinning and weaving were done, as before, on the spinning-wheel and the hand-loom. The Scholfields introduced carding-machinery in place of the hand-cards, and seem to have carried on their business in several places with success. A Scotchman, James Saunderson, who emigrated in 1794, also introduced carding-machines at New Ipswich, N. H., in 1801. Their example, however, was followed by few. Carding-machines were introduced in a few other places between 1800 and 1808 ; but no development of the business of systematically making cloth, or preparing wool for sale, took place. The application of machinery for spinning does not seem to have been made at all.[1] One great difficulty in the way of the woollen manufacture was the deficient supply and poor quality of wool. The means of overcoming this were supplied when in 1802 a large flock of fine merino sheep was imported from Spain,

---

[1] See a sketch of the early history of the woollen manufacture in Taft's "Notes on the Introduction of the Woollen Manufacture." Compare the same writer's account in " Bulletin National Ass. of Wool Manufacturers," II., 478-488 and the scattered notices in Bishop, " Hist. of Manufactures," I., 421, and II., 106, 109, 118, etc.

followed in 1809 and 1810 by several thousand pure me-
rinos from the same country.[1] But imports from England
continued to be large, and those woollen cloths that were
not homespun were obtained almost exclusively from the
mother country.[2]

When the period of restriction began in 1808, the woollen manufacture received, like all other industries in the
same position, a powerful stimulus. The prices of broad-
cloth, then the chief cloth worn besides homespun, rose
enormously, as did those of flannels, blankets, and other
goods, which had previously been obtained almost exclusively by importation. We have no such detailed statements as are given of the rise of the cotton manufacture.
It is clear, however, that the manufacture of woollen
goods, which had had no real existence before, began,
and was considerably extended. The spinning of wool by

---

[1] Bishop, II., 94, 134.

[2] The United States were important customers of woollens for England,
as appears from the following figures, which give in millions of pounds
sterling the total exports of woollens from England, and those of exports to
the United States.

	Total	To the U. S.
1790	5.2	1.5
1791	5.5	1.6
1792	5.5	1.4
1793	3.8	1.0
1794	4.4	1.4
1795	5.2	2.0
1796	6.0	2.3
1797	4.9	1.9
1798	6.5	2.4
1799	6.9	2.8

Brothers, " Wool and Wool Manufactures of Great Britain," 143, 144

machinery was introduced, and goods were made for sale on a large scale. As early as 1810 the carding and spinning of wool by machinery was begun in some of the cotton mills in Rhode Island.[1] In Northampton, Mass., Oriskany, N. Y., and other places, large establishments for the manufacture of woollen goods and of satinets (mixed cotton and woollen goods) sprang up. The value of woollen goods made in factories is said to have risen from $4,000,000 in 1810 to $19,000,000 in 1815.[2]

After 1815 the makers of woollens naturally encountered great difficulties in face of the renewed and heavy importations of English goods. The tariff of 1816 gave them the same duty that was levied on cottons, 25 per cent., to be reduced in three years to 20 per cent. The reduction of the duty to 20 per cent., which was to have taken place in 1819, was then postponed, and in the end never took place. No minimum valuation was fixed for woollen goods; hence there was not, as for cotton goods, a minimum duty. Wool was admitted at a duty of 15 per cent. The scheme of duties, under the tariff of 1816, thus afforded no very vigorous protection. Nor did the provisions of the act of 1824 materially improve the position of the woollen manufacturers. The duty on woollen goods was in that act raised to 30 per cent. in the first instance, and to 33⅓ per cent. after 1825. At the same time the

---

[1] Gallatin's report of 1810, " Am. State Papers, Finance," II. 427 ; Taft, 44.

[2] " Bulletin Wool Manufacturers," II., 486. This is hardly more than a loose, though significant, guess.

duty on wool (except that costing ten cents a pound or less) was raised to 20 per cent. in the first place, to 25 per cent. after 1825, and to 30 per cent. after 1826. If foreign wool had to be imported to supplement the domestic supply,—and such a necessity has constantly existed in this country since 1816,—the increased price of wool in this country, as compared with other countries which admitted wool free or at a lower duty, would tend to make the effectual protection to woollen manufacturers far from excessive.

Notwithstanding the very moderate encouragement given from 1816 to 1828, the woollen manufacture steadily progressed after the crisis of 1819, and in 1828 was securely established. During the years from the close of the war till 1819 much embarrassment was felt, and many establishments were given up; but others tided over this trying time.[1] After 1819 the industry gradually responded to the more favorable influences which then set in for manufactures, and made good progress. During 1821 and 1822 large investments were made in factories for making woollen cloths, especially in New England.[2] In 1823 the manufacturers of woollens in Boston were sufficiently numerous to form an independent

---

[1] Thus a large factory in Northampton, built in 1809 (Bishop, II., 136), was still in operation in 1828 ("Am. State Papers, Finance," V., 815). In Taft's " Notes " there is mention (pp. 39–40) of the Peacedale Manufacturing Company, which began in 1804, and has lasted to the present time. It is said that the spinning-jenny was first applied to wool in this factory.

[2] Bishop, II., 270, 294 ; Niles, XXII., 225.

organization for the promotion of their interests, which were, in that case, to secure higher protective duties.[1] The best evidence which we have of the condition of the industry during these years is to be found in the testimony given in 1828 by various woollen manufacturers before the Committee of the House of Representatives on Manufactures. This testimony shows clearly that the industry was established in 1828 on such a scale that the difficulties arising from lack of skill and experience, unfamiliarity with machinery and methods, and other such temporary obstacles, no longer had influence in preventing its growth.[2] The capital invested by the thirteen manufacturers who testified before this committee varied from $20,000 to $200,000, the average being $85,000. The quantity of wool used by each averaged about 62,000 pounds per year. These figures indicate a scale of operation very considerable for those days. Six of the factories referred to had been established between 1809 and 1815. With the possible exception of one, in regard to which the date of foundation was not stated, none had been established in the years between 1815 and 1820; the remaining six had been built after 1820. Spinning-machinery was in use in all. Some used power-looms, others hand-looms. The application of the power-loom to weaving woollens, said one manufacturer, had been made in the United States

---

[1] Niles, XXV., 148, 189,

[2] The testimony is printed in full in "American State Papers, Finance," V., 792–832.

earlier than in England.[1] An indication, similar to this, of the point reached by the American producers in the use of machinery, was afforded by the difference of opinion in regard to the comparative merits of the jenny, and of the " Brewster," a spinning-machine of recent invention. Goods of various kinds were made—broadcloths, cassimeres, flannels, satinets, and kerseys. The opinion was expressed by several that the mere cost of manufacturing was not greater in the United States than in England ; that the American manufacturer could produce, at as low prices as the English, if he could obtain his wool at as low prices as his foreign competitor.[2] This testi-

---

[1] Testimony, p. 824. The same statement is made by Bishop, II., 317. In Taft's " Notes," p. 39, there is an account of the application of the power-loom to weaving saddle-girths as early as 1814. In 1822 the power-loom for weaving broadcloths seems to have been in common use.—Taft, p. 43.

[2] " Broadcloths are now (1828) made at much less expense of labor and capital than in 1825, by the introduction of a variety of improved and labor-saving machinery, amongst which may be named the dressing-machine and the broad powe -loom of American invention " (p. 824). The power-loom was very generally used. " Since the power-looms have been put in operation, the weaving costs ten cents per yard, instead of from eighteen to twenty-eight cents " (p. 814). Shepherd, of Northampton, to whose factory reference has already been made (*ante* p. 44, note 1), said : " The difference in price of cloths (in the United States and in England) would be the difference in the price of the wool, as, in my opinion, we can manufacture as cheap as they (the English) can " (p. 816). In the same connection another manufacturer said : " The woollen manufacture is not yet fairly established in this country, but I know no reason why we cannot manufacture as well and as cheap as they can in England, except the difference in the price of labor, for which, in my opinion, we are fully compensated by other advantages. Our difficulties are not the cost of manufacturing, but the great fluctuations in the home market, caused by the excessive and irreg-

mony seems to show conclusively that at the time when
it was given the woollen manufacture had reached that
point at which it might be left to sustain itself; at which
accidental or artificial obstacles no longer stood in the
way of its growth. That many of the manufacturers
themselves wanted higher duties, is, for obvious reasons,
not inconsistent with this conclusion. Progress had been
less certain and rapid than in the case of the kindred cotton manufacture, for the conditions of production were
less distinctly favorable. The displacement of the household products by those of the factory was necessarily a
gradual process, and made the advance of the woollen
manufacture normally more slow than that of the kindred
industry. But the growth of the cotton manufacture, so
similar to that of wool, of itself removed many of the obstacles arising from the recent origin of the latter. The
use of machinery became common, and, when the first
great steps had been taken, was transferred with comparative ease from one branch of textile production to
another. In 1828, when for the first time heavy protection was given by a complicated system of minimum duties, and when the actual rates rose, in some cases, to
over 100 per cent., this aid was no longer needed to sus-

---

ular foreign importations. The high prices we pay for labor are, in my
opinion, beneficial to the American manufacturer, as for those wages we
get a much better selection of hands, and those capable and willing to per-
form a much greater amount of labor in a given time. The American manufacturer also uses a larger share of labor-saving machinery than the English " (p. 829).

tain the woollen manufacture. The period of youth had then been past.

It appears that direct protective legislation had even less influence in promoting the introduction and early growth of the woollen than of the cotton manufacture. The events of the period of restriction, from 1808 to 1815, led to the first introduction of the industry, and gave it the first strong impulse. Those events may indeed be considered to have been equivalent to effective, though crude and wasteful, protective legislation, and it may be that their effect, as compared with the absence of growth before 1808, shows that protection in some form was · needed to stimulate the early growth of the woollen manufacture. But, by 1815, the work of establishing the manufacture had been done. The moderate duties of the period from 1816 to 1828, partly neutralized by the duties on wool, may have something to sustain it; but the position gained in 1815 would hardly have been lost in the absence of these duties. By 1828, when strong protection was first given, a secure position had certainly been reached.

V.

THE IRON MANUFACTURE.

WE turn now to the early history of the iron manufacture,—the production of crude iron, pig and bar. We shall examine here the production, not of the finished article, but of the raw material. It is true thát the production of crude iron takes place under somewhat different conditions from those which affect cotton and woollen goods. The production of pig-iron is more in the nature of an extractive industry, and, under ordinary circumstances, is subject in some degree to the law of diminishing returns. To commodities produced under the conditions of that law, the argument for protection to young industries has not been supposed, at least by its more moderate advocates, to apply, since the sites where production will be carried on to best advantage are apt to be determined by unalterable physical causes.[1] It happens, however, that changes in the processes of production, analogous to those which took place in the textile industries, were made at about the same time in the manufacture of crude

---

[1] See, for instance, List, " System of National Economy," Phila., 1856, pp. 296-300.

iron. These changes rendered more possible the successful application of the principle of protection to young industries, and make the discussion of its application more pertinent. There is another reason why we should consider, in this connection, the raw material rather than the finished article. The production of the latter, of the tools and implements made of iron, has not, in general, needed protection in this country, nor has protection often been asked for it. The various industries by which crude iron is worked into tools and consumable articles were firmly established already in the colonial period, and since then have maintained themselves with little difficulty. The controversy on the protection of the iron manufacture has been confined mainly to the production of pig- and bar-iron. It is to this, therefore, that we shall direct our attention. The production of pig- and bar-iron will be meant when, in the following pages, the "iron manufacture" is spoken of.

During the eighteenth century England was a country importing, and not, as she is now, one exporting, crude iron. The production of pig- and bar-iron was accordingly encouraged in her colonies, and production was carried on in them to an extent considerable for those days. Large quantities of bar-iron were exported from the American colonies to England.[1] The manufacture of iron was

[1] See the tables in Bishop, I., 629, and Scrivenor, "History of the Iron Trade," p. 81. In 1740 the total quantity of iron produced in England was about 17,000 tons ; at that time from 2,000 to 3,000 tons annually were regularly imported from the American colonies.

firmly established in the colonies according to the methods common at the time. During the second half of the eighteenth century, however, the great change took place in England in the production of iron which has placed that country in its present position among iron-making countries, and has exercised so important an influence on the material progress of our time. Up to that time charcoal had been used exclusively for smelting iron, and the iron manufacture had tended to fix itself in countries where wood was abundant, like Norway, Sweden, Russia, and the American colonies. About 1750 the use of coke in the blast furnace began. The means were thus given for producing iron in practically unlimited quantities, without dependence for fuel on forests easily exhaustible; and in the latter part of the century, when the steam-engine supplied the motive power for the necessary strong blast, production by means of coke increased with great rapidity.[1] At the same time, in 1783 and 1784, came the inventions of Cort for puddling and rolling iron. By these the transformation of pig-iron into bar-iron of convenient sizes was effected in large quantities. Before the inventions of Cort, pig-iron had been first converted into bar under the hammer, and the bar, at a second distinct operation in a slitting mill, converted into bars and rods of convenient size. The rolled bar made by the processes of puddling and rolling—which are still in common use—is

---

[1] See the good account of the importance of the use of coke (coal) in Jevons, " The Coal Question," ch. XV., pp. 309-316.

inferior in quality, at least after the first rolling, to the hammered and slit iron, known as hammered bar, produced by the old method. Cort's processes, however, made the iron much more easily and cheaply, and the lower price of the rolled iron more than compensated, for most purposes, for its inferior quality. At the same time these processes made easy and fostered the change from production on a small sale to production on a large scale. This tended to bring about still greater cheapness, and made the revolution in the production of iron as great as that in the textile industries, and similar to it in many important respects.

During the period 1789-1808 these changes in the iron manufacture were too recent to have had any appreciable effect on the conditions of production and supply in the United States. The manufacture of iron, and its transformation into implements of various kinds, went on without change from the methods of the colonial period. Pig-iron continued to be made and converted into hammered bar in small and scattered works and forges.[1]   No pig-iron seems to have been imported. Bar-iron was imported, in quantities not inconsiderable, from Russia[2]; but no crude iron was imported from England. The importations of certain iron articles, not much advanced beyond the crude state, such as nails, spikes, anchors, cables, showed a perceptible increase during this period.[3]

---

[1] French, "Hist. of Iron Manufacture," p. 16.   [2] *Ibid.*, p. 13.

[3] The imports of iron, so far as separately stated in the Treasury reports, may be found in Young's Report on Tariff Legislation, pp. XXVI.-XXXVI. Cp. Grosvenor, "Does Protection Protect?" pp. 174, 175.

Whether this increase was the result of the general conditions which tended to swell imports during this period,
or was the first effect of the new position which England
was taking as an iron-making country, cannot be determined.   Information on the state of the industry during
this period is meagre ; but it seems to have been little
affected by the protective duties which Congress enacted
on nails, steel, and some other articles.   No protection
was attempted to be given to the production of pig or
bar-iron, for it was thought that the domestic producers
would be able to compete successfully with their foreign
competitors in this branch of the iron-trade.

During the period of restriction from 1808 to 1815, the
iron and manufactures of iron previously imported, had
to be obtained, as far as possible, at home.   A large increase in the quantity of iron made in the country accordingly took place.   The course of events was so similar to
that already described in regard to textile manufactures
that it need not be referred to at length.   When peace
came, there were unusually heavy importations of iron,
prices fell rapidly, and the producers had to go through
a period of severe depression.

In 1816 Congress was asked to extend protection to
the manufacture of iron, as well as to other industries.
The tariff of 1816 imposed a duty of 45 cents a hundred-
weight on hammered-bar iron, and one of $1.50 a hun-
dred-weight on rolled bar, with corresponding duties on
sheet, hoop, and rod iron.   Pig-iron was admitted under

an *ad valorem* duty of 20 per cent. At the prices of bar-iron in 1816, the specific duty on hammered bar was equivalent to about 20 per cent.,[1] and was, therefore, but little higher than the rates of 15 and 17½ per cent. levied in 1804 and 1807. The duty on rolled bar was much higher, relatively to price, as well as absolutely, than that on hammered bar, and was the only one of the iron duties of 1816 which gave distinct and vigorous protection. These duties were not found sufficient to prevent the manufacturers from suffering heavy losses, and more effective protection was demanded. In 1818, Congress, by a special act, raised the duties on iron considerably, at the same time, as was noted above,[2] that it postponed the reduction from 25 to 20 per cent. on the duty on cottons and woollens. Both of these measures were concessions to protective feeling, and they may have been the result of an uneasy consciousness of the disturbed state of the country and of the demand for protection which was to follow the financial crisis of the next year.[3] The act of 1818 fixed the duty on pig-iron at 50 cents per hundred-weight—the first specific duty imposed on pig-iron; hammered bar was charged with 75 cents a hundred-weight, instead of 45 cents, as in 1816; and higher duties were put on castings, anchors, nails, and spikes.[4] These duties

---

[1] See the tables of prices in French, pp. 35, 36.

[2] *Ante*, p. 27.

[3] There is nothing in the Congressional debates on the acts of 1818 to show what motives caused them to be passed.

[4] "Statutes at Large," III., 460.

were comparatively heavy ; and with a steady fall in the
price of iron, especially after the crisis of 1818–19, they
became proportionately heavier and heavier.   Nevertheless, in the tariff of 1824 they were further increased.
The rate on hammered bar went up to 90 cents a hundred-
weight ; that on rolled bar still remained at $1.50, as it
had been fixed in 1816.   In 1828 a still further increase
was made in the specific duties on all kinds of iron, although the continual fall in prices was of itself steadily
increasing the weight of the specific duties.   The duty on
pig-iron went up to 62½ cents a hundred-weight ; that on
hammered bar to a cent a pound (that is, $1.12 a hundred-
weight); that on rolled bar to $37 a ton.   In 1832 duties
were reduced in the main to the level of those of 1824, and
in 1833 the Compromise Act, after maintaining the duties
of 1832 for two years, gradually reduced them still further,
till in 1842 they reached a uniform level of 20 per cent.   On
the whole, it is clear that after 1818 a system of increasingly
heavy protection was applied to the iron manufacture,
and that for twenty years this protection was maintained
without a break.   From 1818 till 1837 or 1838, when the
reduction of duty under the Compromise Act began to
take effect to an appreciable extent, the duties on iron in
its various forms ranged from 40 to 100 per cent. on the
value.

It is worth while to dwell for a moment on the heavy
duty on rolled iron—much higher than that on hammered
iron—which was adopted in 1816, and maintained through-

out this period. Congress attempted to ward off the competition of the cheaper rolled iron by this heavy discriminating duty, which in 1828 was equivalent to one hundred per cent. on the value. When first established in 1816, the discrimination was defended on the ground that the rolled iron was of inferior quality, and that the importation of the unserviceable article should be impeded for the benefit of the consumer. The scope of the change in the iron manufacture, of which the appearance of rolled iron was one sign, was hardly understood in 1816 and 1818, and this argument against its use may have represented truthfully the animus of the discriminating duty. But in later years the wish to protect the consumer from impositions hardly continued to be the motive for retaining the duty. Rolled bar-iron soon became a well-known article, of considerable importance in commerce. The discriminating duty was retained throughout, and in 1828 even increased ; it was still levied in the tariff of 1832 ; it reappeared when the Whigs carried the tariff of 1842 ; and it did not finally disappear till 1846. The real motive for maintaining the heavy tax through these years undoubtedly was the unwillingness of the domestic producers to face the competition of the cheaper article. The tax is a clear illustration of that tendency to fetter and impede the progress of improvement which is inherent in protective legislation. It laid a considerable burden on the community, and, as we shall see, it was of no service in encouraging the early growth of the iron industry. It is curious to note that the same contest against improved processes was carried on in France, by a discriminating duty on English rolled iron, levied first in 1816, and not taken off till 1860.[1]

After 1815 the iron-makers of the United States met with strong foreign competition from two directions. In the first place, English pig and rolled iron was being produced with steadily decreasing cost. The use of coke became universal in England, and improvements in methods of production were constantly made. Charcoal continued to be used exclusively in the furnaces of this country; for the possibility of using anthracite had not yet been discovered, and the bituminous coal fields lay too far from what was then the region of dense population to be available. While coke-iron was thus driving out charcoal-iron for all purposes for which the former could be used, the production of charcoal-iron itself encountered the competition of Sweden and Russia. As the United States advanced in population, the more accessible forests became exhausted, and the greater quantity of charcoal-iron needed with the increase of population and of production, could be obtained at home only at higher cost. The Scandinavian countries and Russia, with large forests and a population content with low returns for labor, in large part supplied the increased quantity at lower rates than the iron-makers of this country. Hence the imports of iron show a steady increase, both those of pig-iron and

---

[1] Amé, "Études sur les Tarifs de Douanes," I., 145.

and those of rolled and hammered bar; the rolled bar coming from England, and the hammered bar from Sweden and Russia. The demand for iron was increasing at a rapid rate, and there was room for an increase both of the domestic production and of imports; but the rise in imports was marked. Notwithstanding the heavy duties, the proportion of imported to domestic iron from 1818 to 1840 remained about the same.[1]

Since importations continued regularly and on a considerable scale, the price of the iron made at home was clearly raised, at the seaboard, over the price of the foreign iron by the amount of the duty. The country, therefore, paid the iron tax probably on the greater part used, whether of foreign or domestic origin, in the shape of prices from forty to one hundred per cent. higher than those at which the iron could have been bought abroad.

---

[1] On the production and imports of iron in the years after 1830 the reader is referred to the remarks on p. 124, and to the " Quarterly Journal of Economics," vol. II., p. 377. Until the middle of the decade 1820–30 the annual product of pig-iron is supposed to have been about 50,000 tons, while in the second half of the decade it is put at 100,000 tons and more. The imports of crude iron averaged about 20,000 tons per year in 1818–21, about 30,000 tons in 1822–27, and rose to an average of about 40,000 tons in 1828–30. These figures as to imports refer mainly to bar-iron ; and as it required in those days about $1\frac{2}{8}$ tons of pig to make a ton of bar (French, p. 54), some additions must be made to the imports of bar before a proper comparison can be made between the domestic and the imported supply. An addition must also be made for the considerable imports of steel, sheet-iron, anvils, anchors, and other forms of manufactured iron. Figures of imports are given in Grosvenor, pp. 198, 199 ; of domestic production, by R. W. Raymond, in A. S. Hewitt's pamphlet on " A Century of Mining and Metallurgy," page 31.

The fact that the manufacture, notwithstanding the heavy and long-continued protection which it enjoyed, was unable to supply the country with the iron which it needed, is of itself sufficient evidence that its protection as a young industry was not successful.   It is an essential condition for the usefulness of assistance given to a young industry, that the industry shall ultimately supply its products at least as cheaply as they can be obtained by importation ; and this the iron manufacture failed to do. There is, however, more direct evidence than this, that the manufacture was slow to make improvements in production, which might have enabled it eventually to furnish the whole supply needed by the country, and in this way might have justified the heavy taxes laid for its benefit.   Pig-iron continued to be made only with charcoal.   The process of puddling did not begin to be introduced before 1830, and then inefficiently and on a small scale.[1]   Not until the decade between 1830 and 1840, at a time when the Compromise Act of 1833 was steadily decreasing duties, was puddling generally introduced.[2]   The iron rails needed for the railroads built at this time—the first parts of the present railroad system—were supplied exclusively by importation.   In 1832 an act of Congress had provided that duties should be refunded on all imported rails laid down within three years from the date

---

[1] See an excellent article, by an advocate of protection, in the *American Quarterly Review*, Vol. IX. (1831), pp. 376, 379, which gives very full information in regard to the state of the iron manufacture at that date.

[2] French, p. 56.

of importation. Under this act all the first railroads imported their rails without payment of duty. Finally, the great change which put the iron manufacture on a firm and durable basis did not come till the end of the decade 1830-40, when all industry was much depressed, and duties had nearly reached their lowest point. That change consisted in the use of anthracite coal in the blast-furnace. A patent for smelting iron with anthracite was taken out in 1833; the process was first used successfully in 1836. In 1838 and 1839 anthracite began to be widely used. The importance of the discovery was promptly recognized; it was largely adopted in the next decade, and led, among other causes, to the rapid increase of the production of iron, which has been so often ascribed exclusively to the protection of the tariff of 1842. With this change the growth of the iron manufacture on a great scale properly begins.[1]

It seems clear that no connection can be traced between the introduction and early progress of the iron manufacture, and protective legislation. During the colonial period, as we have seen, under the old system of production of iron, the country had exported and not imported iron. The production of charcoal-iron and of hammered bar was carried on before the adoption of the Constitution. During the first twenty years after 1789, the iron-makers

---

[1] Swank's Report on "Iron and Steel Production," in the Census of 1880, p. 114. A fuller discussion of the introduction of the use of anthracite, and of the effect of protective duties after this had been done, will be found at pages 122-134.

still held their own, although the progress of invention elsewhere, and the general tendency in favor of heavy imports, caused a growing importation from abroad. The production of iron by the old methods and with the use of charcoal was therefore in no sense a new industry. If the business of making charcoal-iron could not be carried on or increased during this and the subsequent period, the cause must have lain in natural obstacles and disadvantages which no protection could remove. After 1815, the new régime in the iron trade had begun; the use of coke in the blast-furnace, and the production of wrought-iron by puddling and rolling, had changed completely the conditions of production. The protective legislation which began in 1818, and continued in force for nearly twenty years, was intended, it is true, to ward off rather than to encourage the adoption of the new methods; but it is conceivable that, contrary to the intentions of its authors, it might have had the latter effect. No such effect, however, is to be seen. During the first ten or fifteen years after the application of protection, no changes of any kind took place. Late in the protective period, and at a time when duties were becoming smaller, the puddling process was introduced. The great change which marks the turning-point in the history of the iron manufacture in the United States—the use of anthracite—began when protection ceased. It is probably not true, as is asserted by advocates of free trade,[1] that protection had

---

[1] *E. g.*, Grosvenor, p. 197.

any appreciable influence in retarding the use of coal in making iron. Other causes, mainly the refractory nature of the fuel, sufficiently account for the failure to use anthracite at an earlier date. The successful attempts to use anthracite were made almost simultaneously in England and in the United States.[1] The failure to use coke from bituminous coal, which had been employed in England for over half-a-century, was the result of the distance of the bituminous coal-fields from the centre of population, and of the absence of the facility of transportation which has since been given by railroads. It is hardly probable, therefore, that protection exercised any considerable harmful influence in retarding the progress of improvement. But it is clear, on the other hand, that no advantages were obtained from protection in stimulating progress. No change was made during the period of protection which enabled the country to obtain the metal more cheaply than by importation, or even as cheaply. The duties simply taxed the community; they did not serve to stimulate the industry, though they probably did not appreciably retard its growth. We may therefore conclude that the duties on iron during the generation after 1815 formed a heavy tax on consumers; that they impeded, so far as they went, the industrial development of the country; and that no compensatory benefits were obtained to offset these disadvantages.

[1] Swank, pp. 114, 115.

VI.

CONCLUDING REMARKS.

THE three most important branches of industry to which protection has been applied, have now been examined. It has appeared that the introduction of the cotton manufacture took place before the era of protection, and that—looking aside from the anomalous conditions of the period of restriction from 1808 to 1815—its early progress, though perhaps somewhat promoted by the minimum duty of 1816, would hardly have been much retarded in the absence of protective duties. The manufacture of woollens received little direct assistance before it reached that stage at which it could maintain itself without help, if it were for the advantage of the country that it should be maintained. In the iron manufacture twenty years of heavy protection did not materially alter the proportion of home and foreign supply, and brought about no change in methods of production. It is not possible, and hardly necessary, to carry the inquiry much further. Detailed accounts cannot be obtained of other industries to which protection was applied; but so far as can be seen, the same course of events took place in them as in the three whose history we have followed. The same general conditions affected the manufactures of glass, earthenware, paper, cotton-bagging, sail-duck, cordage, and other articles to which protection was applied during this time with more or less vigor. We may assume that the same general effect, or absence of effect, followed in these as in the other cases. It is not intended to speak of the production of agricultural commodities like sugar, wool, hemp, and flax, to which also protection was applied. In the production of these the natural advantages of one country over another tell more decidedly and surely than in the case of most manufactures, and it has not often been supposed that they come within the scope of the argument we are considering.

Although, therefore, the conditions existed under which it is most likely that protection to young industries may be advantageously applied—a young and undeveloped country in a stage of transition from a purely agricultural to a more diversified industrial condition; this transition, moreover, coinciding in time with great changes in the arts, which made the establishment of new industries peculiarly difficult—notwithstanding the presence of these conditions, little, if any thing, was gained by the protection which the United States maintained in the first part of this century. Two causes account for this. On the one hand, the character of the people rendered the transition of productive forces to manufactures comparatively easy; on the other hand, the shock to economic habits during the restrictive period from 1808 to 1815 effectually prepared the way for such a transition. The genius of the people for mechanical arts showed itself early. Naturally it appeared with most striking results in those fields in which the circumstances of the country gave the richest opportunities; as in the application of steam-power to navigation, in the invention and improvement of tools, and especially of agricultural implements, and in the cotton manufacture. The ingenuity and inventiveness of American mechanics have become traditional, and the names of Whitney and Fulton need only be mentioned to show that these qualities were not lacking at the time we are considering. The presence of such men rendered it more easy to remove the obstacles arising from want of skill and experience in manufactures. The political institutions, the high average of intelligence, the habitual freedom of movement from place to place and from occupation to occupation, also made the rise of the existing system of manufacturing production at once more easy and less dangerous than the same change in other countries. At the same time it so happened that the embargo, the non-intercourse acts, and the war of 1812 rudely shook the country out of the grooves in which it was running, and brought about a state of confusion from which the new industrial system could emerge more easily than from a well-settled organization of industry. The restrictive period may indeed be considered to have been one of extreme protection. The stimulus which it gave to some manufactures perhaps shows that the first steps in these were not taken without some artificial help. The intrinsic soundness of the argument for protection to young industries therefore may not be touched by the conclusions drawn from the history of its trial in the United States, which shows only that the intentional protection of the tariffs of 1816, 1824, and 1828 had little effect. The period from 1808 till the financial crisis of 1818–19 was a disturbed and chaotic one, from which the country settled down, with little assistance from protective legislation, into a new arrangement of its productive forces.

The system of protective legislation began in 1816, and was maintained till toward the end of the decade 1830–40. The Compromise Act of 1833 gradually undermined it. By 1842 duties reached a lower point than that from which they had started in 1816. During this whole period the argument for protection to young industries had been essentially the mainstay of the advocates of protection, and the eventual cheapness of the goods was the chief advantage which they proposed to obtain. It goes without saying that this was not the only argument used, and that it was often expressed loosely in connection with other arguments. One does not find in the popular discussions of fifty years ago, more than in those of the present, precision of thought or expression. The "home market" argument, which, though essentially distinct from that for

young industries, naturally suggests itself in connection
with the latter, was much urged during the period we are
considering.   The events of the War of 1812 had vividly
impressed on the minds of the people the possible inconvenience, in case of war, of depending on foreign trade
for the supply of articles of common use; this point also
was much urged by the protectionists.   Similarly the
want of reciprocity, and the possibility of securing, by retaliation, a relaxation of the restrictive legislation of foreign countries, were often mentioned.   But any one who
is familiar with the protective literature of that day,—as
illustrated, for instance, in the columns of " Niles's Register,"—cannot fail to note the prominent place held by the
young-industries argument.   The form in which it most
commonly appears is in the assertion that protection normally causes the prices of the protected articles to fall, [1] an
assertion which was supposed, then as now, to be sufficiently supported by the general tendency toward a fall in
the price of manufactured articles, consequent on the great
improvement in the methods of producing such articles.

Shortly after 1832, the movement in favor of protection, which had had full sway in the Northern States since
1820, began to lose strength.   The young-industries

---

[1] See, for instance, the temperate report of J. Q. Adams, in 1832, in
which this is discussed as the chief argument of the protectionists.   Adams,
though himself a protectionist, refutes it, and bases his faith in protection
chiefly on the loss and inconvenience suffered through the interruption of
foreign trade in time of war.   The report is in " Reports of Committees,
22d Congress, 1st Session, vol. V., No. 481.

argument at the same time began to be less steadily pressed. About 1840 the protective controversy took a new turn. It seems to have been felt by this time that manufactures had ceased to be young industries, and that the argument for their protection as such, was no longer conclusive. Another position was taken. The argument was advanced that American labor should be protected from the competition of less highly paid foreign labor. The labor argument had hardly been heard in the period which has been treated in the preceding pages. Indeed, the difference between the rate of wages in the United States and in Europe, had furnished, during the early period, an argument for the free-traders, and not for the protectionists. The free-traders were then accustomed to point to the higher wages of labor in the United States as an insuperable obstacle to the successful establishment of manufactures. They used the wages argument as a foil to the young-industries argument, asserting that as long as wages were so much lower in Europe, manufacturers would not be able to maintain themselves without aid from the government. The protectionists, on the other hand, felt called on to explain away the difference of wages; they endeavored to show that this difference was not so great as was commonly supposed, and that, so far as it existed, it afforded no good reason against adopting protection.[1] About 1840, the positions of the con-

---

[1] See, among others, Clay's Tariff Speech of 1824, "Works," I., 465, 466.

tending parties began to change.[1] The protectionists began to take the offensive on the labor question: the free-
traders were forced to the defensive on this point. The
protectionists asserted that high duties were necessary to
shut out the competition of the ill-paid laborers of Europe, and to maintain the high wages of the laborers of the
United States. Their opponents had to explain and de-
fend on the wages question. Obviously this change in the
line of argument indicates a change in the industrial situation. Such an argument in favor of protection could not
have arisen at a time when protective duties existed but in
small degree, and when wages nevertheless were high. Its
use implies the existence of industries which are supposed
to be dependent on high duties. When the protective
system had been in force for some time, and a body of industries had sprung up which were thought to be able to
pay current wages only if aided by high duties, the wages
argument naturally suggested itself. The fact that the

[1] Same signs of the appeal for the benefit of labor appear as early as 1831
in a passage in Gallatin's " Memorial," p. 31, and again in a speech of Webster's in 1833, " Works," I., 283. In the campaign of 1840, little was
heard of it, doubtless because other issues than protection were in the
foreground. Yet Calhoun was led to make a keen answer to it in a speech
of 1840, " Works," III., 434. In the debates on the tariff act of 1842, we
hear more of it ; see the speeches of Choate and Buchanan, *Congr. Globe*,
1841-42, pp. 950, 953, and Calhoun's allusion to Choate, in Calhoun's
" Works," IV., 207. In 1846 the argument appeared full-fledged, in the
speeches of Winthrop, Davis, and others, *Congr. Globe*, 1846, Appendix.
pp , 967, 973, 1114. See also a characteristic letter in Niles, vol. 62, p.
262. Webster's speech in 1846, " Works," V., 231, had much about protection and labor, but in a form somewhat different from that of the argument we are nowadays familiar with.

iron manufacture, which had hitherto played no great part in the protective controversy, became, after 1840, the most prominent applicant for aid, accounts in large part for the new aspect of the controversy. The use of the wages argument, and the rise of the economic school of Henry C. Carey, show that the argument for young industries was felt to be no longer sufficient to be the mainstay of the protective system. The economic situation had changed, and the discussion of the tariff underwent a corresponding change.

THE EARLY PROTECTIVE MOVEMENT
AND THE TARIFF OF 1828.

In the present essay we shall consider, not so much the economic effect of the tariff, as the character of the early protective movement and its effect on political events and on legislation.

The protective movement in this country has been said to date from the year 1789, even from before 1789; and more frequently it has been said to begin with the tariff act of 1816. But whatever may have been, in earlier years, the utterances of individual public men, or the occasional drift of an uncertain public opinion, no strong popular movement for protection can be traced before the crisis of 1818-19. The act of 1816, which is generally said to mark the beginning of a distinctly protective policy in this country, belongs rather to the earlier series of acts, beginning with that of 1789, than to the group of acts of 1824, 1828, and 1832. Its highest permanent rate of duty was twenty per cent., an increase over the previous rates which is chiefly accounted for by the heavy interest charge on the debt incurred during the war. But after the crash of 1819, a movement in favor of protection set in, which was backed by a strong popular feeling such as had been absent in the earlier years. The causes of the new movement are not far to seek. On the one hand there was a great collapse in the prices of land and of agricultural products, which had been much inflated during the years from 1815 to 1818. At the same time the foreign market for grain and provisions, which had been highly profitable during the time of the Napoleonic wars, and which there had been a spasmodic attempt to regain for two or three years after the close of our war in 1815, was almost entirely lost. On the other hand, a large number of manufacturing industries had grown up, still in the early stages of growth, and still beset with difficulties, yet likely in the end to hold their own and to prosper. That disposition to seek a remedy from legislation, which always shows itself after an industrial crisis, now led the farmers to ask for a home market, while the manufacturers wanted protection for young industries. The distress that followed the crisis brought out a plentiful crop of pamphlets in favor of protection, of societies and conventions for the promotion of domestic industry, of petitions and memorials to Congress for higher duties. The movement undoubtedly had deep root in the feelings and convictions of the people, and the powerful hold which protective ideas then obtained influenced the policy of the nation long after the immediate effects of the crisis had ceased to be felt.[1]

---

[1] The character of the protective movement after 1819 is best illustrated by the numerous pamphlets of Matthew Cary. See especially the " Appeal

The first effect of this movement was seen in a series
of measures which were proposed and earnestly pushed
in Congress in the session of 1819–20. They included a
bill for a general increase of duties, one for shortening
credits on duties, and one for taxing sales by auction of
imported goods. The first of these very nearly took an
important place in our history, for it was passed by the
House, and failed to pass the Senate by but a single vote.
Although it did not become law, the protective movement
which was expressed in the votes and speeches on it remained unchanged for several years, and brought about
the act of 1824, while making possible the act of 1828.
Some understanding of the state of feeling in the different sections of the country is necessary before the peculiar
events of 1828 can be made clear, and it may be conven-
iently reached at this point.

The stronghold of the protective movement was in the
Middle and Western states of those days—in New York,
New Jersey, Pennsylvania, Ohio, and Kentucky. They
were the great agricultural States ; they felt most keenly
the loss of the foreign market of the early years of the
century, and were appealed to most directly by the cry for a
home market. At the same time they had been most deep-
ly involved in the inflation of the years 1816–19, and were
in that condition of general distress and confusion which

to Common Sense and Common Justice " (1822) and " The Crisis : A Sol-
emn Appeal," etc. (1823). " Niles's Register," which had said little about
tariff before 1819, thereafter became a tireless and effective advocate of
protection.

leads people to look for some panacea. The idea of protection as a cure for their troubles had obtained a strong hold on their minds. It is not surprising, when we consider the impetuous character of the element in American democracy at that time represented by them, that the idea was applied in a sweeping and indiscriminate manner. They wanted protection not only for the manufactures that were to bring them a home market, but for many of their own products, such as wool, hemp, flax, even for wheat and corn. For the two last mentioned they asked aid more particularly in the form of higher duties on rum and brandy, which were supposed to compete with spirits distilled from home-grown grain. A duty on molasses was a natural supplement to that on rum. Iron was already produced to a considerable extent in Pennsylvania and New Jersey, and for that also protection was asked.

In New England there was a strong opposition to many of these demands. The business community of New England was still made up mainly of importers, dealers in foreign goods, shipping merchants, and vessel-owners, who naturally looked with aversion at measures that tended to lessen the volume of foreign trade. Moreover, they had special objections to many of the duties asked for by the agricultural states. Hemp in the form of cordage, flax in the form of sail duck, and iron, were important items in the cost of building and equipping ships. The duties on molasses and rum were aimed at an industry carried on almost exclusively in New England :

the importation of molasses from the West Indies in exchange for fish, provisions, and lumber, and its subsequent manufacture into rum. Wool was the raw material of a rapidly growing manufacture. So far the circumstances led to opposition to the protective movement. On the other hand, the manufacture of cotton and woollen goods was increasing rapidly and steadily, and was the moving force of a current in favor of protection that became stronger year by year. We have seen that the beginning of New England's manufacturing career dates back to the War of 1812. Before 1820 she was fairly launched on it, and between 1820 and 1830 she made enormous advances. The manufacturers carried on a conflict, unequal at first, but rapidly becoming less unequal, with the merchants and ship-owners. As early as 1820 Connecticut and Rhode Island were pretty firmly protective; but Massachusetts hesitated. Under the first weight of the crisis of 1819, the protective feeling was strong enough to cause a majority of her congressmen to vote for the bill of 1820. But there was great opposition to that bill, and after 1820 the protective feeling died down.[1] In 1824 Massachusetts was still disinclined to adopt the protective system, and it was not until the end of the decade that she came

---

[1] The vote on the bill of 1820, by States, is given in Niles, XVIII., 169. Of the Massachusetts members 19 voted yes, 6 no, and 4 were absent. Of the New England members 19 voted yes, 9 no, and 9 were absent. The opposition to the bill in Massachusetts was the occasion of a meeting at which Webster made his first speech on tariff, which is not reprinted in his works, but may be found in the newspapers of the day.

squarely in line with the agricultural states on that subject.

The South took its stand against the protective system with a promptness and decision characteristic of the political history of the slave states. The opposition of the Southern members to the tariff bill of 1820 is significant of the change in the nature of the protective movement between 1816 and 1820. The Southern leaders had advocated the passage of the act of 1816, but they bitterly opposed the bill of 1820. It is possible that the Missouri Compromise struggle had opened their eyes to the connection between slavery and free trade.[1] At all events, they had grasped the fact that slavery made the growth of manufactures in the South impossible, that manufactured goods must be bought in Europe or in the North, and that, wherever bought, a protective tariff would tend to make them dearer. Moreover, Cotton was not yet King, and the South was not sure that its staple was indispensable for all the world. While the export of cotton on a large scale had begun, it was feared that England, in retaliation for high duties on English goods, might tax or exclude American cotton.

Such was in 1820 the feeling in regard to the protective system in the different parts of the country. After the failure of the bill of that year, the movement for higher duties seems for a while to have lost headway. The low-

---

[1] But no reference was made to the Missouri struggle in the debates on the tariff bill of 1820.

est point of industrial and commercial depression, so far as indicated by the revenue, was reached at the close of 1820, and, as affairs began to mend, protective measures received less vigorous support. Bills to increase duties, similar to the bill of 1820, were introduced in Congress in 1821 and 1822, but they were not pressed and led to no legislation.[1]

Public opinion in most of the Northern States, however, continued to favor protection ; the more so because, after the first shock of the crisis of 1819 was over, recovery, though steady, was slow. As a Presidential election approached and caused public men to respond more readily to popular feeling, the protectionists gained a decided victory. The tariff of 1824 was passed, the first and the most direct fruit of the early protective movement. The Presidential election of that year undoubtedly had an effect in causing its passage ; but the influence of politics and political ambition was in this case hardly a harmful one. Not only Clay, the sponsor of the American System, but Adams, Crawford, and Jackson were declared advocates of protection. Party lines, so far as they existed at all, were not regarded in the vote on the tariff. It was carried mainly by the votes of the Western and Middle

---

[1] See the interesting account of a Cabinet meeting in November, 1821, in "J. Q. Adams's Memoirs," vol. V., pp. 408-411. "The lowest point of the depression was reached at the close of last year" [1820]. Calhoun thought "the prosperity of the manufacturers was now so clearly established that it might be mentioned in the message as a subject for congratulation." Crawford said "there would not be much trouble in the ensuing session with the manufacturing interest," and Adams himself "had no apprehension that there would be much debate on manufacturing interests."

states. The South was in opposition, New England was divided ; Rhode Island and Connecticut voted for the bill, Massachusetts and the other New England states were decidedly opposed.[1]

The opposition of Massachusetts was the natural result of the character of the new tariff. The most important changes made by it were in the increased duties on iron, lead, wool, hemp, cotton-bagging, and other articles whose protection was desired chiefly by the Middle and Western States. The duties on textile fabrics, it is true, were also raised. Those on cotton and woollen goods went up from 25 to 33⅓ per cent. This increase, however, was offset, so far as woollens were concerned, by the imposition of a duty of 30 per cent. on wool, which had before been admitted at 15 per cent. The manufacturers of woollen goods were, therefore, as far as the tariff was concerned, in about the same position as before.[2] The heavier duties

---

[1] John Randolph said, in his vigorous fashion, of the tariff bill of 1824 : " The merchants and manufacturers of Massachusetts and New Hampshire repel this bill, while men in hunting shirts, with deerskin leggings and moccasins on their feet, want protection from home manufactures."—" Debates of Congress, 1824, p. 2370.

[2] This can be shown very easily. The cost of the wool is about one half the cost of making woollen goods. Then we have in 1816 :

Duty on woollens	25	per cent.
Deduct duty on wool, ½ of 15 cent.	7½	"
Net protection in 1816	17½	"

And in 1824 we have:

Duty on woollens	33⅓	per cent.
Deduct duty on wool, ½ of 30 per cent.	15	"
Net protection in 1824	18⅓	"

The rise in duties both on wool and on woollens took place gradually by the terms of the act of 1824. The calculation is based on the final rates, which were reached in 1826.

on iron and hemp, on the other hand, were injurious to the ship-builders.

The manufacture of textiles was rapidly extending in all the New England States. At first that of cottons received most attention, and played the most important part in the protective controversy. But by 1824 the cotton industry was firmly established and almost independent of support by duties. The woollen manufacture was in a less firm position, and in 1824 became the prominent candidate for protection. Between 1824 and 1828 a strong movement set in for higher duties on woollens, which led eventually to some of the most striking features of the tariff act of 1828.

The duties proposed and finally established on woollens were modelled on the minimum duty of 1816 on cottons. By the tariff act of that year, it will be remembered, cotton goods were made subject to a general *ad valorem* duty of 25 per cent. ; but it was further provided that " all cotton cloths, whose value shall be less than 25 cents per square yard, shall be taken and deemed to have cost 25 cents per square yard, and shall be charged with duty accordingly." That is, a specific duty of six and a quarter cents a square yard was imposed on all cotton cloths costing twenty-five cents a square yard or less. The minimum duties, originally intended to affect chiefly East Indian goods and goods made from East Indian cotton, had an effect in practice mainly on goods from England, whether made of American or of Indian cotton. In a few

years, as the use of the power loom and other improvements in manufacture brought the price of coarse cottons
much below twenty-five cents, the minimum duties became prohibitory. How far they were needed in order to
promote the success and prosperity of the cotton manufacture in years following their imposition, we have
already discussed.[1] At all events, whether or not in
consequence of the duties, large profits were made by
those who entered on it, and in a few years the cheaper
grades of cotton cloth were produced so cheaply, and of
such good quality, that the manufacturers freely asserted
that the duty had become nominal, and that foreign competition no longer was feared.

This example had its effect on the manufacturers of
woollen goods, and on the advocates of protection in general. In the tariff bill of 1820, minimum duties on linen
and on other goods had been proposed. In 1824 an earnest effort was made to extend the minimum system to
woollens. The committee which reported the tariff bill
of that year recommended the adoption in regard to
woollens of a proviso framed after that of the tariff of
1816 in regard to cottons, the minimum valuation being
eighty cents a yard. The House first lowered the valuation to forty cents and finally struck out the whole proviso
by a scant majority of three votes.[2] There was one great
obstacle in the way of a high duty on cheap woollen

---

[1] See above, pp. 25–36.
[2] The vote was 104 to 101. "Annals of Congress," 1823–24, p. 2310.

goods: they were imported largely for the use of slaves on Southern plantations. Tender treatment of the peculiar institution had already begun, and there was strong opposition to a duty which had the appearance of being aimed against the slave-holders. The application of the minimum principle to other than cheap woollen goods apparently had not yet been thought of; but the idea was obvious, and soon was brought forward.

After 1824 there was another lull in the agitation for protection. Trade was buoyant in 1825, and production profitable. For the first time since 1818 there was a swing in business operations. This seems to have been particularly the case with the woollen manufacturers. During the years from 1815 to 1818–19, they, like other manufacturers, had met with great difficulties; and when the first shock of the crisis of the latter year was over, matters began to mend but slowly. About 1824, however, according to the accounts both of their friends and of their opponents on the tariff question, they extended their operations largely.[1] It is clear that this expansion, such as it was, was not the effect of any stimulus given by the tariff of 1824, for, as we have seen, the encouragement given the woollen manufacturers by that act was no greater than had been given under the act of 1816. At all events, the upward movement lasted but a short time.

---

[1] See the Report of the Harrisburg Convention of 1827 in Niles, XXXIII., 109; Tibbits, "Essay on Home Market" (1827), pp. 26, 27; Henry Lee, "Boston Report of 1827," pp. 64 *seq*.

In England a similar movement had been carried to the extreme of speculation and had resulted in the crisis of 1825–26. From England the panic was communicated to the United States; but, as the speculative movement had not been carried so far in this country, the revulsion was less severely felt. It seems, however, to have fallen on the woollen manufacturers with peculiar weight. Parliament, it so happened, in 1824 had abolished almost entirely the duty on wool imported into England. It went down from twelve pence to one penny a pound.[1] The imports of woollen goods into the United States had in 1825 been unusually large ; the markets were well stocked; the English manufacturers were at once enabled to sell cheaply by the lower price of their raw material, and pushed to do so by the depression of trade.

A vigorous effort was now made to secure legislative aid to the woollen makers, similar to that given the cotton manufacturers. Massachusetts was the chief seat of the woollen industry. The woollen manufacturers held meetings in Boston and united for common action, and it was determined to ask Congress to extend the minimum sys-

---

[1] It is sometimes said that this reduction of the wool duty in England was undertaken with the express purpose of counteracting the protective duties imposed on woollens in the United States. But there is little ground for supposing that our duties were watched so vigilantly in England, or were the chief occasion for English legislation. The agitation for getting rid of the restriction on the import and export of wool began as early as 1819, and during its course very little reference, if any, was made to the American duties. See the sketch in Bischoff's " History of the Woollen and Worsted Manufactures," vol. II., chapters 1 and 2.

tem to woollen goods.[1] The legislature of the State passed resolutions asking for further protection for woollens, and these resolutions were presented in the federal House of Representatives by Webster.[2] A deputation of manufacturers was sent to Washington to present the case to the committee on manufactures. Their efforts promised to be successful. When Congress met for the session of 1826–27, the committee (which in those days had charge of tariff legislation) reported a bill which gave the manufacturers all they asked for.

This measure contained the provisions which, when finally put in force in the tariff of 1828, became the object of the most violent attack by the opponents of protection. It made no change in the nominal rate of duty, which was to remain at 33⅓ per cent. But minimum valuations were added, on the plan of the minima on cottons, in such a way as to carry the actual duty far beyond the point indicated by the nominal rate. The bill provided that all goods costing less than 40 cents a square yard were to pay duty as if they had cost 40 cents; all costing more than 40 cents and less than $2.50 were to be charged as if they had cost $2.50; all costing between $2.50 and $4.00 to be charged as if they had cost $4.00. A similar

---

[1] The memorial of the manufacturers to Congress is in Niles, XXXI., 185. It asks for minimum duties, on the ground that *ad valorem* duties are fraudulently evaded. For the circular sent out by this committee, see *ibid.*, p. 200.

[2] "American State Papers, Finance," V., 599 ; " Annals of Congress," 1826–27, p. 1010.

course was proposed in regard to raw wool. The *ad valorem* rate on raw wool was to be 30 per cent. in the first place, and to rise by steps to 40 per cent.; and it was to be charged on all wool costing between 16 cents and 40 cents a pound as if the wool had cost 40 cents. The effect of this somewhat complicated machinery was evidently to levy specific duties both on wool and on woollens. On wool the duty was to be, eventually, 16 cents a pound. On woollens it was to be 13⅓ cents a yard on woollens of the first class, 83⅓ cents on those of the second class, and $1.33⅓ on those of the third class.

The minimum system, applied in this way, imposed *ad valorem* duties in form, specific duties in fact. It had some of the disadvantages of both systems. It offered temptations to fraudulent undervaluation stronger than those offered by *ad valorem* duties. For example, under the bill of 1827, the duty on goods worth in the neighborhood of 40 cents a yard would be 13⅓ cents if the value was less than 40 cents ; but if the value was more than 40 cents, the duty would be 83⅓ cents. If the value could be made to appear less than forty cents, the importer saved 70 cents a yard in duties. Similarly, at the next step in the minimum points, the duty was 83⅓ cents if the goods were worth less than $2.50, and $1.33⅓ cents if the goods were worth more than $2.50. The temptation to undervalue was obviously very strong under such a system, in the case of all goods which could be brought with any plausibility near one of the minimum points.

On the other hand, the system had the want of elasticity which goes with specific duties. All goods costing between 40 cents and $2.50 were charged with the same duty, so that cheap goods were taxed at a higher rate than dear goods. The great gap between the first and second minimum points (40 cents and $2.50) made this objection the stronger. But that gap was not the result of accident. It was intended to bring about a very heavy duty on goods of the grade chiefly manufactured in this country. The most important domestic goods were worth about a dollar a yard, and their makers, under this bill, would get a protective duty of $83\frac{1}{3}$ cents a yard. The object was to secure a very high duty, while retaining nominally the existing rate of $33\frac{1}{3}$ per cent.

The woollens bill of 1827 had a fate similar to that of the general tariff bill of 1820. It was passed in the House, but lost in the Senate by the casting vote of the Vice-President. In the House the Massachusetts members, with one exception, voted for it, and both Senators from Massachusetts supported it.[1]

This bill having failed, the advocates of protection determined to continue their agitation, and to give it wider scope. A national convention of protectionists was determined on.[2] Meetings were held in the different States

---

[1] " Congressional Debates," III., 1099, 496.

[2] It is not very clear in what quarter the scheme of holding such a convention had its origin. The first public suggestion came from the Philadelphia Society for the Promotion of Domestic Industry, an association founded by Hamilton, of which Matthew Carey and C. J. Ingersoll were at this time the leading spirits.

in which the protective policy was popular, and delegates were appointed to a general convention. In midsummer of 1827 about a hundred persons assembled at Harrisburg, and held the Harrisburg convention, well known in its day. Most of the delegates were manufacturers, some were newspaper editors and pamphleteers, a few were politicians.[1] The convention did not confine its attention to wool and woollens. It considered all the industries which were supposed to need protection. It recommended higher duties for the aid of agriculture ; others on manufactures of cotton, hemp, flax, iron, and glass ; and finally, new duties on wool and woollens. The movement was primarily for the aid of the woollen industry ; other interests were included in it as a means of gaining strength. The duties which were demanded on woollens were on the same plan as those proposed in the bill of 1827, differing only in that they were higher. The *ad valorem* rate on woollen goods was to be 40 per cent. in the first place, and was to be raised gradually until it reached 50 per cent. It was to be assessed on minimum valuations of fifty cents, two dollars and a half, four dollars, and six dollars a yard. The duty on wool was to be twenty cents a pound in the first instance, and was to be raised each year by $2\frac{1}{2}$ cents until it should reach fifty cents a pound. Needless to say, the duty would be pro-

---

[1] Among the politicians was Mallary of Vermont, who had been chairman of the committee on manufactures in the preceding Congress, and became the spokesman of the protectionists in the ensuing session, when the tariff of 1828 was passed.

hibitory long before this limit was reached. Wool costing less than eight cents was to be admitted free.[1]

At this point a new factor, which we may call " politics,"
began to make itself felt in the protective movement.
The natural pressure of public opinion on public men had
exercised its effect in previous years, and had had its
share in bringing about the tariff act of 1824 and the
woollens bill of 1827. But the gradual crystallization of
two parties, the Adams and Jackson parties,—Whigs and
Democrats, as they soon came to be called—put a new
face on the political situation, and had an unexpected
effect on tariff legislation. The contest between them
had begun in earnest before the Harrisburg convention
met, and some of the Jackson men alleged that the convention was no more than a demonstration got up by the
Adams men as a means of bringing the protective movement to bear in their aid ; but this was denied, and such
evidence as we have seems to support the denial.[2]   Yet

---

[1] The proceedings of the convention, the address of the people, the memorial to Congress, etc., are in Niles, XXXII. and XXXIII.

[2] I have been able to find little direct evidence as to the political bearing
of the Harrisburg convention.   Matthew Carey, in a letter of July, 1827,
while admitting he is an Adams man, protests against " amalgamating the
question of the presidency with that for the protection of manufactures."
Niles, XXXII., 389. The (New York) *Evening Post*, a Jackson paper,
said the convention was a manœuvre of the Adams men ; see its issues of
August 1 and August 9, 1827.   This was denied in the *National Intelligencer* (Adams) of July 9th, and also in the (New York) *American* (Adams) of
July 9th.   The *Evening Post* admitted (August 11th) that " doubtless many
members of the convention were innocent of political views," and that " the
rest were induced to postpone or abandon their political views."   Van
Buren apparently suspected that the convention might have a political

the Adams men were undoubtedly helped by the protective movement. Although there was not then, nor for a number of years after, a clear-cut division on party lines between protectionists and so-called free traders, the Adams men were more firmly and unitedly in favor of protection than their opponents. Adams was a protectionist, though not an extreme one; Clay, the leader and spokesman of the party, was more than any other public man identified. with the American system. They were at least willing that the protective question should be brought into the foreground of the political contest.[1]

The position of the Jackson men, on the other hand,

meaning, and warned its members against forming "a political cabal"; *cf.* the *National Intelligencer* of July 26th. But among the delegates from New York were both Jackson and Adams men. See Hammond, "Political History of New York," II., 256–258; Niles, XXXII., 349. Niles, who was an active member of the convention, denied strenuously that politics had any thing to do with it. Niles, XXXIV., 187.—Since the above was put in type, however, a letter of Clay's has been found which seems to indicate that the movement for holding such a convention was at least started by the anti-Jackson leaders. The letter is printed in the " Quarterly Journal of Economics," vol. II., July, 1888.

[1] There is ground for suspecting that the Adams party would have been willing to make the tariff question the decisive issue of the presidential campaign. Clay made it the burden of his speeches during his journey to the West in the early summer of 1827. Very soon after this, however, the correspondence between Jackson and Carter Beverly was published, and fixed attention on the " bargain and corruption " cry. That was the point which the Jackson managers succeeded in making most prominent in the campaign. Clay dropped the question of protection ; he found enough to do in answering the charge that in 1825 a corrupt bargain had made Adams President and himself Secretary of State. See Clay's speech at Pittsburg. June 20, 1827, in Niles, XXXII., 299. On June 29th, Clay published his first denial of the " bargain and corruption " charges. *Ibid.*, p. 350. *Cf.* Parton, " Life of Jackson," III., 111.

was a very difficult one.   Their party had at this time no
settled policy in regard to the questions which were to be
the subjects of the political struggles of the next twenty
years.   They were united on only one point, a determi-
nation to oust the other side.   On the tariff, as well as on
the bank and internal improvements, the various elements
of the party held very different opinions.   The Southern
members, who were almost to a man supporters of Jackson, were opposed unconditionally not only to an increase
of duties, but to the high range which the tariff had already reached.   They were convinced, and in the main
justly convinced, that the taxes levied by the tariff fell
with peculiar weight on the slave States, and their opposition was already tinged with the bitterness which made
possible, a few years later, the attempt at nullification of
the tariff of 1832.   On the other hand, the protective
policy was popular throughout the North, more especially
in the very States whose votes were essential to Jackson,
in New York, Pennsylvania, and Ohio.   The Jackson men
needed the votes of these States, and were not so confi-
dent of getting them as they might reasonably have been.
They failed, as completely as their opponents, to gauge
the strength of the enthusiasm of the masses for their
candidate, and they did not venture to give the Adams
men a chance of posing as the only true friends of domestic industry.

The twentieth Congress met for its first session in
December, 1827.   The elections of 1826, at which its

members were chosen, had not been fortunate for the administration. When Congress met there was some doubt
as to the political complexion of the House; but this was
set at rest by the election to the speakership of the Democratic candidate, Stephenson of Virginia.[1] The new
Speaker, in the formation of the committees, assumed for
his party the direction of the measures of the House. On
the committee on manufactures, from which the tariff
report and the tariff bill were to come, he appointed five
supporters of Jackson and two supporters of Adams. The
chairmanship, however, was given to one of the latter,
Mallary, of Vermont, who, it will be remembered, had
been a member of the Harrisburg convention.

Much doubt was entertained as to the line of action the
committee would follow. The Adams men feared at first
that it would adopt a policy of simple delay and inaction.
This fear was confirmed when, a few weeks after the
beginning of the session, the committee asked for power
to send for persons and papers in order to obtain more
information on the tariff,—a request which was opposed
by Mallary, their chairman, on the ground that it was
made only as a pretext for delay. The Adams men, who
formed the bulk of the ardent protectionists, voted with
him against granting the desired power. But the Southern members united with the Jackson men from the

---

[1] Stephenson's election is said to have been brought about by Van
Buren's influence; Parton, "Life of Jackson," III., 135. It is worth
while to bear this in mind, in view of the part played by Van Buren later
in the session.

North, and between them they secured the passage of the resolution asked by the committee.[1]   The debate and vote on the resolution sounded the key-note of the events of the session.   They showed that the Jackson men from the South and the North, though opposed to each other on the tariff question, were yet united as against the Adams men.[2]

But the policy of delay, if such in fact had been entertained by the opposition, was abandoned.   On January 31st, the committee presented a report and a draft of a tariff bill, which showed that they had determined on a new plan, and an ingenious one.   What that plan was, Calhoun explained very frankly nine years later, in a speech reviewing the events of 1828 and defending the course taken by himself and his Southern fellow-members.[3]   A high-tariff bill was to be laid before the House.   It was to contain not only a high general range of duties, but duties especially high on those raw materials on which New England wanted the duties to be low.   It was to satisfy the protective demands of the Western and Middle States, and at the same time to be obnoxious to the New England members.   The Jackson men of all shades, the protectionists from the North and the free-traders from

---

[1] The power granted to the committee by this resolution, to examine witnesses, was used to a moderate extent.   A dozen wool manufacturers were examined, and their testimony throws some light on the state of the woollen manufacture at that time.   See the preceding essay, pp. 42–44.

[2] In "Congressional Debates," IV., 862, 870.

[3] Speech of 1837 ; "Works," III., 46–51.

the South, were to unite in preventing any amendments; that bill, and no other, was to be voted on. When the final vote came, the Southern men were to turn around and vote against their own measure. The New England men, and the Adams men in general, would be unable to swallow it, and would also vote against it. Combined, they would prevent its passage, even though the Jackson men from the North voted for it. The result expected was that no tariff bill at all would be passed during the session, which was the object of the Southern wing of the opposition. On the other hand, the obloquy of defeating it would be cast on the Adams party, which was the object of the Jacksonians of the North. The tariff bill would be defeated, and yet the Jackson men would be able to parade as the true "friends of domestic industry."

The bill by which this ingenious solution of the difficulties of the opposition was to be reached, was reported to the House on January 31st by the committee on manufactures.[1] To the surprise of its authors, it was eventually passed both by House and Senate, and became, with a few unessential changes, the tariff act of 1828.

The committee's bill in the first place proposed a large increase of duties on almost all raw materials. The duty on pig-iron was to go up from 56 to 62½ cents per hundredweight, that on hammered bar-iron from 90 to 112 cents per hundredweight, and that on rolled bar from $30

---

[1] The bill as reported by the committee is printed in "Congressional Debates," IV., 1727 :

to $37 per ton. The increase on hammered bar had been asked by the Harrisburg convention. But on pig and on rolled bar no one had asked for an increase, not even the manufacturers of iron who had testified before the committee.[1]

The most important of the proposed duties on raw materials, however, were on hemp, flax, and wool. The existing duty on hemp was $35 per ton. It was proposed to increase it immediately to $45, and further to increase it by an annual increment of $5, till it should finally reach $60. Hemp of coarse quality was largely raised in the country at that time, especially in Kentucky. It was suitable for the making of common ropes and of cotton bagging, and for those purposes met with no competition from imported hemp. Better hemp, suitable for making cordage and cables, was not raised in the country at all, the supply coming exclusively from importation. The preparation of this better quality (" water-rotted " hemp) required so much manual labor, and labor of so disagreeable a character, that it would not have been undertaken in any event by the hemp growers of this country.[2]

---

[1] See the testimony of the three iron manufacturers who were examined, " American State Papers, Finance," V., 784–792. Mallary, in introducing the bill, said : " The committee gave the manufacturer of iron all he asked, even more." "Congressional Debates," IV., 1748.

[2] Gallatin, " Memorial of the Free-Trade Convention " (1831), p. 51. This admirable paper, perhaps the best investigation on tariff subjects ever made in the United States, is unfortunately not reprinted in the edition of Gallatin's collected works. The original pamphlet is very scarce. The memorial is printed in U. S. Documents, 1st session, 22d Congress, Senate Documents, vol. I., No. 55.

Under such conditions an increase of duty on hemp could be of no benefit to the American grower. Its effect would be simply to burden the rope-makers and the users of cordage, and ultimately the ship-builders and ship-owners. Essentially the same state of things has continued to our own day. The high duties on hemp, which have been maintained from the outset to the present time, have never succeeded in checking a large and continuous importation. The facts were then, and are now, very similar with flax; yet the same duty of $60 per ton was to be put on flax.

On wool a proposal of a similar kind was made. The duty under the tariff of 1824 had been 30 per cent. This was to be changed to a mixed specific and *ad valorem* duty, the first mixed duty ever enacted in the United States. Wool was to pay seven cents a pound (this was reduced to four cents in the act as finally passed), and in addition 40 per cent. in 1828, 45 per cent. in 1829, and thereafter 50 per cent. The object of the mixed duty was to make sure that a heavy tax should be put on coarse wool. The coarse wool, used in the manufacture of carpets and of some cheap flannels and cloths, was not then grown in the United States to any extent, and, indeed, has been grown at no time in this country, but has always been imported, mainly from Asia Minor and from South America. Its cost at the place of exportation was in 1828 from four to ten cents a pound.[1] The

---

[1] Gallatin, "Memorial," p. 67.

price being so low, a simple *ad valorem* duty would not have affected it much.   But the additional specific duty of seven (four) cents weighted it heavily.   The *ad valorem* part of the duty reached the higher grades of wool, which were raised in this country ; it was calculated to please the farmer.   The specific part reached the lower grades, which were not raised in this country, and was calculated to annoy and embarrass the manufacturers.   This double object, and especially the second half of it, the Jackson men wanted to attain, and for that reason the policy of admitting the cheap wool at low rates was set aside,—a policy which has been followed in all our protective tariffs, with the sole exception of that of 1828.[1]

Another characteristic part of the scheme was the handling of those duties on woollens that corresponded to the duties on cheap wool.   It had been customary to fix low duties on the coarse woollen goods made from cheap wool, partly because of the low duty on the wool

---

[1] It was followed in 1824, 1832, 1842, and again in the wool and woollens act of 1867, on which the existing duties [1887] are based.   The rates on wool have been :

	1828	1832	1842	1867
General duty on wool	30 per cent.	4c. plus 40 per cent.	3c. plus 30 per cent.	10c.–12c. plus 11 per cent.
Duty on cheap wool	15 per cent. on wool under 10c.	free, wool under 8c.	5 per cent. on wool under 7c.	3c. on wool under 12c.

itself, and partly because coarse woollens were used largely for slaves on Southern plantations. Thus in 1824 woollen goods costing less than 33⅓ cents a yard had been ad-mitted at a duty of 25 per cent., while woollens in general paid 33⅓ per cent. In 1828 this low duty on coarse woollens was continued, although the wool of which they were made was subject for the first time to a heavy duty. The object again was to embarrass the manufacturers, and make the bill unpalatable to the protectionists and the Adams men.

The same object appeared in the duty on molasses, which was to be doubled, going from five to ten cents a gallon. A spiteful proviso was added in regard to the drawback which it had been customary to allow on the exportation of rum distilled from imported molasses. The bill of 1828, and the act as finally passed, expressly refused all drawbacks on rum; the intention obviously being to irritate the New Englanders. The animus ap-peared again in the heavy duty on sail-duck, and the re-fusal of drawback on sail-duck exported by vessels in small quantities for their own use.[1]

In the duties on woollen goods the changes from the schedule proposed by the Harrisburg convention were on the surface not very great; but in reality they were im-portant. The committee gave up all pretence of *ad*

---

[1] Sail-duck was charged 9 cents a yard, with an increase of ½ cent yearly, until the duty should finally be 12½ cents. This was equivalent to 40 or 50 per cent. In 1824 the duty had been 15 per cent. Drawback was refused on any quantity less than 50 bolts exported in one vessel at one time.

valorem duties. This was not an insignificant circumstance; for the *ad valorem* rate of the minimum system was said by its opponents to be no more than a device for disguising the heavy duties actually levied under it. The committee brushed aside this device, and made the duties on woollens specific and unambiguous. On goods costing 50 cents a square yard or less, the duty was 16 cents; on goods costing between 50 cents and \$1.00, 40 cents; on those costing between \$1.00 and \$2.50, \$1.00; and on those costing between \$2.50 and \$4.00, \$1.60. Goods costing more than \$4.00 were to pay 45 per cent. These specific duties, it will be seen, were the same as if an *ad valorem* duty of 40 per cent. had been assessed, on the minimum principle, on valuations of 50 cents, \$1.00, \$2.50, and \$4.00. The changes from the Harrisburg convention scheme were, therefore, the arrangement of specific duties in such a way that they were equivalent to an *ad valorem* rate of but 40 per cent. (the convention had asked 50 per cent.); and, next, the insertion of a minimum point of \$1.00, the Harrisburg scheme having allowed no break between 40 cents and \$2.50. The first change might have been submitted to by the protectionists; but the second was like putting a knife between the crevices of their armor. We have already noted the importance of the gap between the minimum points of 40 cents and \$2.50. A very large part of the imported goods were worth, abroad, in the neighborhood of \$1.00; and the largest branch of the domestic manufacture made goods of the same character and value. The original scheme had given a very heavy duty, practically a prohibitory duty, on these goods, while the new scheme gave a comparatively insignificant duty of 40 cents. As one of the protectionists said : " The dollar minimum was planted in the very midst of the woollen trade." [1]

The bill, in fact, was ingeniously framed with the intention of circumventing the Adams men, especially those from New England. The heavy duties on iron, hemp, flax and wool were bitter pills for them. The new dollar minimum took the life out of their scheme of duties on woollen goods. The molasses and sail-duck duties, and the refusal of drawbacks on rum and duck, were undisguised blows at New England. At the same time, some of these very features, especially the hemp, wool, and iron duties, served to make the bill popular in the Western and Middle States, and made opposition to it awkward for the Adams men. The whole scheme was a characteristic product of the politicians who were then becoming prominent as the leaders of the Democracy, men of a type very different from the statesmen of the preceding generation. Clay informs us that it was one of the many devices that had their origin in the fertile brain of Van

---

[1] " Congressional Debates," IV., 2274. See the statement of the effect of the minimum system in " State Papers," 1827–28, No. 143. Davis (of Massachusetts) said that the minimum of $1.00 " falls at a point the most favorable that could be fixed for the British manufacturer. * * * It falls into the centre of the great body of American business." " Congressional Debates," IV., 1894, 1895. See to the same effect the speech of Silas Wright, *Ibid.*, p. 1867.

Buren.[1] Calhoun said in 1837 that the compact between
the Southern members and the Jackson leaders had come
about mainly through Silas Wright; and Wright made
no denial.[2]

The result of this curious complication of wishes and
motives was seen when the tariff bill was finally taken up
in the House in March.   Mallary, as chairman of the committee on manufactures, introduced and explained the
bill.   Being an Adams man, he was of course opposed to
it, and moved to amend by inserting the scheme of the
Harrisburg convention.   The amendment was rejected
by decisive votes, 102 to 75 in committee of the whole,[3]
and 114 to 80 in the House. The majority which defeated

---

[1] " I have heard, without vouching for the fact, that it [the tariff of 1828]
was so framed on the advice of a prominent citizen, now abroad [Van Buren had been made minister to England in 1831], with the view of ultimately defeating the bill, and with assurances that, being altogether unac-
ceptable to the friends of the American system, the bill would be lost."
Clay's speech of February, 1832.   " Works " II., 13.

[2] See Calhoun's speech of 1837, as cited above, p. 88.   In the debate of
1837, Wright admitted the compact with the Southern members, but said
that he had warned them that the New England men in the end might
swallow the obnoxious bill. " Congressional Debates," XIII., 922, 926–927.
Wright was a member of the committee on manufactures, was the spokesman of the Jackson men who formed the majority of its members, and had
charge of the measure before the House. Jenkins, " Life of Wright,"
pp. 53–60.

The Adams men saw through the scheme at the time.   Clay wrote to J.
J. Crittenden, in February, even before the House began the discussion of
the bill : " The Jackson party are playing a game of brag on the subject of
the tariff.   They do not really desire the success of their own measure ;
and it may happen in the sequel that what is desired by neither party will
command the votes of both."   " Life of Crittenden," I., 67.

[3] " Congressional Debates," IV., 2038.

the amendment was composed of all the Southern members, and of the Jackson members from the North, chiefly from New York, Pennsylvania, Ohio, and Kentucky. The minority consisted almost exclusively of friends of the administration.[1] Mallary then moved to substitute that part only of the Harrisburg convention scheme which fixed the duties on wool and woollens ; that is, the original minimum scheme, with a uniform duty of forty per cent. on wool. This too was rejected, but by a narrow vote, 98 to 97.[2] The Jackson men permitted only one change of any moment: they reduced the specific duty on raw wool from seven cents, the point fixed by the committee, to four cents, the *ad valorem* rate remaining at 40 per cent.[3] The duty on molasses was retained, by the same combination that refused to accept the Harrisburg scheme.[4] The Southern members openly said that they meant to make the tariff so bitter a pill that no New England member would be able to swallow it.[5]

---

[1] See Niles, XXXV., 57, where the various votes on the bill are ananalyzed. The vote on Mallary's amendment was ;

    Yeas .   .   . 78 Adams men, 2 Jackson men .   .   . 80
    Nays . . . 14 " " 100 " " . . . 114
[2] "Congressional Debates," IV., 2050.
[3] The Adams men seem to have opposed this reduction. The vote was :
    Yeas .   .   . 10 Adams men, 90 Jackson men .   .   . 100
    Nays . . . 79 " " 20 " " . . . 99
[4] On reducing the molasses duty, the vote was :
    Yeas .   .   . 72 Adams men, 10 Jackson men .   .   . 82
    Nays . . . 19 " " 95 " " . . . 114
[5] Most of the Southern members kept silence during the debates on the details of the bill. After its third reading, McDuffie and others made long speeches against it. One of the South Carolina Congressmen, however,

When the final vote on the bill came, the groups of members split up in the way expected by the Democrats. The Southern members, practically without exception, voted against it. Those from the Middle and Western States voted almost unanimously for it. The Jackson men voted for their own measure for consistency's sake ; the Adams men from these States joined them, partly for political reasons, mainly because the bill, even with the obnoxious provisions, was acceptable to their constituents. Of the New England members, a majority, 23 out of 39, voted in the negative. The affirmative votes from New England, however, were sufficient, when added to those from the West and the Middle States, to ensure its passage. The bill accordingly passed the House.[1]

This result had not been entirely unexpected. The real struggle, it was felt, would come in the Senate, where the South and New England had a proportionately large representation. In previous years the Senate had maintained, in its action on the tariff bills of 1820 and 1824, a

said frankly : " He should vote for retaining the duty on molasses, because he believed that keeping it in the bill would get votes against its final passage" "Congressional Debates," IV., 2349. The Jackson free-traders from the North (there were a few such) followed the same policy. See Cambreleng's remarks, *ibid.*, 3326. See also the passage quoted in Niles, XXXV., 52.

[1] The vote was :

Yeas	61 Adams men,	44 Jackson men		105
Nays	35 "	" 59	" "	94

If six of those New England members who voted yea, had voted nay, the bill would have failed. Niles, *loc. cit.*

much more conservative position than the House.[1] But in 1828 the course of events in the Senate was in the main similar to that in the House. The bill was referred to the committee on manufactures, and was returned with amendments, of which the most important referred to the duty on molasses and to the duties on woollen goods. The duty on molasses was to be reduced from 10 cents, the rate fixed by the House, to $7\frac{1}{2}$ cents. The duties on woollen goods, in the bill as passed by the House, had been made specific, equivalent to 40 per cent. on minimum valuations of 50 cents, $1.00, $2.50, and $4.00. The Senate committee's amendment made the duties *ad valorem* in form, to be assessed on the minimum valuation just mentioned. The rate was to be 40 per cent. for the first year; thereafter, 45 per cent.[2]

---

[1] The tariff of 1824 was much changed in the Senate from the shape in which it had been passed by the House. "Annals of Congress," 1823–24, pp. 723–735.

[2] It was expected that this change to *ad valorem* duties would have still another effect. According to the method then in use for assessing *ad valorem* duties, the dutiable value of goods imported from Europe was ascertained by adding 10 per cent. to the cost or invoice value. See the act of 1828, "Statutes at Large," IV., 274, substantially re-enacting the provisions of the revenue-collection act of 1789, "Statutes at Large," I., 141. It was expected that by the force of this provision the effect of the *ad valorem* rate, under the Senate amendment, would be to increase the duty not merely to 45 per cent., but to $49\frac{1}{2}$ per cent. Hence Webster, in his speech on the bill, spoke of the amendment as carrying the duty "up to 45 or perhaps 50 per cent. *ad valorem*." "Works," III., 231. But the Secretary of the Treasury, Rush, finally decided, very properly, that the provision did not apply to duties assessed on minimum valuations, thereby causing much dissatisfaction among the protectionists. See "Congressional Debates," VI., 802.

Other amendments were proposed, all tending to make the bill less objectionable to the New England Senators. Most of them were rejected. The proposed reduction on molasses was rejected by the same combination that had prevented the reduction from being made in the House. The Southern Senators, and those from the North who supported Jackson, united to retain the duty of 10 cents. When Webster moved to reduce the duty on hemp, only the New England Senators voted with him. Again, an attempt was made to increase the duty on coarse woollens, on which, it will be remembered, the House had put a low rate, notwithstanding the heavy duty on coarse wool. The Senate, by a strict party vote, retained the duty as the House had fixed it. One of the amendments, however, was carried—that which changed the duties on woollens to an *ad valorem* rate of 45 per cent. Two Democratic Senators, Van Buren and Woodbury, who had voted with the South against other amendments, voted in favor of this one. It was carried by a vote of 24 to 22, while all others had been rejected by a vote of 22 to 24.[1]

With this amendment, the bill was finally passed by the Senate, the vote being 26 to 21. The Southern Senators (except two from Kentucky, and one each from Tennessee and Louisiana) voted against it.. Those from the Middle and Western States all voted for it. Those from New England split; six voted yea, five nay. The result

---

[1] The votes in the Senate are given in Niles, XXXIV., 178, 179, 196.

seems to have depended largely on Webster. His colleague Silsbee voted nay, and Webster himself had been in doubt a week before the final vote.[1] Finally he swallowed the bill; and he carried with him enough of the New England Senators to ensure its passage.

Webster defended his course to his constituents on the ground that the woollens amendment (fixing the 45 per cent. *ad valorem* rate) had made the bill much more favorable to the manufacturers. He said he should not have voted for it in the shape in which the House passed it.[2] Calhoun made the same statement in 1837, in the speech to which reference has already been made.[3] No doubt the slight change on woollens mollified in some degree the New England men ; but after all, political motives, or, as Webster put it, " other paramount considerations," caused them to swallow the bill. They were afraid to reject it, for fear of the effect in the approaching campaign and election.[4]

---

[1] " Memoirs of J. Q. Adams," VII., 530, 534.

[2] In a speech made a month later ; printed in his " Works," I., 165. In the House, the representative from Boston had voted against the bill, and Webster commended his action. In his Senate speech Webster had said that, even at the 45 per cent. rate, the duty on woollens was barely sufficient to compensate for the duty on wool. " Works," III., 241.

[3] " Works," III., 50, 51. Calhoun even accused Van Buren of being the "real author" of the tariff of 1828. He said that, but for Van Buren's vote in favor of the woollens amendment, there would have been a tie on the amendment ; his own casting vote as Vice-President would have defeated it ; the bill, without the amendment, would have been rejected by Webster and the other New England Senators. Therefore, Van Buren was responsible for its having been passed.

[4] After the final vote in the House, John Randolph said : " The bill re-

· The act of 1828 had thus been passed in a form approved by no one. It was hardly to be expected that a measure of this kind should long remain on the statute-book, and it was superseded by the act of 1832. During the intervening four years several causes combined to lead to more moderate application of the protective principle. The protective feeling diminished. Public opinion in the North had been wellnigh unanimous in favor of protection between 1824 and 1828; but after 1828, although there was still a large preponderance for protection,[1] there was a strong and active minority against it. The tariff question ceased to be an important factor in politics, so that this obstacle to its straightforward treatment was removed. And, finally, there was a strong desire to make

ferred to manufactures of no sort or kind, except the manufacture of a President of the United States." In 1833, Root, a representative from New York, said : "The act of 1828 he had heard called the bill of Abominations. . . . It certainly grew out of causes connected with President-making. It was fastened on the country in the scuffle to continue the then incumbent in office, on one side, and on the other to oust him and put another in his stead. . . . The public weal was disregarded, and the only question was : Shall we put A or B in the presidential chair ? When it was thought necessary to secure a certain State in favor of the then incumbent, a convention was called at Harrisburg to buy them over. [See, however, the note to p. 84, above.] On the other side another convention was called, who mounted the same hobby. The price offered was the same on both sides : a high tariff. One candidate was thought to be a favorite, because he was supposed to be a warm friend of the protective system, and would support a high tariff ; but they were told, on the other side, that their candidate would go for as high a tariff." "Congressional Debates," IX., 1104, 1105.

[1] As Gallatin admits: "It is certain that at this time (1832) the tariff system is supported by a majority of the people and of both Houses of Congress." "Works," II., 455.

some concession to the growing opposition of the South. It is true that in 1832 Clay and the more extreme protectionists wished to retain the act of 1828 intact, and to effect reductions in the revenue by lowering the non-protective duties only.[1] But most of the protectionists, led by Adams, took a more moderate course, and consented to the removal of the abominations of 1828.

Even before 1832 some changes were made. In 1830 the molasses abomination was got rid of. The duty on molasses was reduced from ten cents a gallon to five cents, the rate imposed before 1828, and the drawback on exportation of rum was restored.[2] At the same time the duties on tea, coffee, and cocoa were lowered, as one means of reducing the revenue.[3]

The most important step taken in 1832 was the entire abolition of the minimum system. Woollen goods were subjected to a simple *ad valorem* duty of 50 per cent. The minimum system, as arranged in the act of 1828, had been found to work badly. The manufacturers said it had been positively injurious to them.[4] As might have been expected, it led to attempts at evasion of duties, to undervaluation, and to constant disputes at the cus-

---

[1] "Works," I., 586–595.

[2] "Statutes at Large," IV., 419. The act seems to have passed without debate or opposition.

[3] *Ibid.*, p. 403.

[4] Browne, of Boston, a manufacturer who had actively supported the minimum system, declared: "I could manufacture to better advantage under the tariff of 1816 than under that of 1828; for the duty on wool was then lower, and that on cloths a better protection." Niles XLI., 204.

tom-houses. The troubles arose mainly under the dollar minimum. Goods worth $1.25 or $1.50 were invoiced so as to bring their values below $1.00, in order to escape the duty under the next minimum point, $2.50. The difficulties were ascribed to the depravity of foreign exporting houses and to the laxity of the revenue laws, and in 1830 a special act in regard to goods made of cotton or wool was passed, making more stringent the provisions for collecting duties. But the troubles continued nevertheless,[1] and, in truth, they were inevitable under a system which imposed specific duties graded according to the value of the goods. Similar duties exist in the present tariff (1887) on some classes of wool and woollens, and lead to the same unceasing complaints of dishonesty and fraud, and the same efforts to make the law effective by close inspection and severer penalties. In 1832, the protectionists themselves swept away the minimum system. The *ad valorem* duty of 50 per cent. which was put in its place was left to be not without its

---

[1] "Statutes at Large," IV., 400. See the speeches of Mallary, "Congressional Debates," VI., 795–803, and of Davis, *ibid.*, p. 874, for instances and proofs of the frauds. The act provided for forfeiture of goods fraudulently undervalued; but no verdicts under it could be obtained. At the protectionist convention held in New York in 1831, one of the speakers said: "The same mistaken current of opinion which prevailed on 'change, entered and influenced the jury-box. Men thought the law rigorous and severe. They considered it hard that a man should forfeit a large amount of property for a mere attempt to evade an enormous duty. In two years there was but a single case pursued into a court of justice." Niles, XLI., 203. See also the Report on Revenue Frauds, made by a committee of this same convention, in Niles, XLI., Appendix, p. 33.

dangers in the matter of fraud and under-valuation, but it was harmless as compared with the minimum system of 1828.[1]

The other "abominations" of the act of 1828 were also done away with in 1832. The duty on hemp, which had been $60 a ton in 1828, was reduced to a duty of $40. Flax, which had also been subjected to a duty of $60 a ton in 1828, was put on the free list. The duties on pig- and bar-iron were put back to the rates of 1824. The duty on wool alone remained substantially as it had been in 1828, being left as a compound duty of 4 cents a pound and 40 per cent. But even here the special abomination of 1828 was removed; cheap wool, costing less than 8 cents a pound, was admitted free of duty. In fact, the protective system was put back, in the main, to where it had been in 1824. The result was to clear the tariff of the excrescences which had grown on it in 1828, and to put it in a form in which the protectionists could advo-cate its permanent retention.

Even in this modified form, however, the system could not stand against the attacks of the South. In the fol-lowing year, 1833, the compromise tariff was passed. It provided for a gradual and steady reduction of duties. That reduction took place; and in July, 1842, a general

---

[1] J. Q. Adams, who was most active in framing the act of 1832, tried to embody the " home valuation" principle into it ; but in vain. " Congres-sional Debates," VIII., 3658, 3671. He also tried to give the government an option to take goods on its own account at a slight advance over the declared value ; but this plan also was rejected. *Ibid.*, p. 3779.

level of 20 per cent. was reached.   Two months later, in September, 1842, a new tariff act, again of distinctly protective character, went into effect.   But this act belongs to a different period, and has a different character from the acts of 1824, 1828, and 1832.   The early protective movement, which began in 1819, and was the cause of the legislation of the following decade, lost its vigor after 1832.   Strong popular sentiment in favor of protection wellnigh disappeared, and the revival of protection in 1842 was due to causes different from those that brought about the earlier acts.   The change in popular feeling is readily explained.   The primary object of the protective legislation of the earlier period had been attained in 1842.   The movement was, after all, only an effort, half conscious of its aim, to make more easy the transition from the state of simple agriculture and commerce which prevailed before the war of 1812, to the more diversified condition which the operation of economic forces was reasonably certain to bring about after 1815.   The period of transition was passed, certainly by 1830, probably earlier.   At all events, very soon after 1820 it was felt that there was not the same occasion as in previous years for measures to tide it over, and a decline in the protective feeling was the natural consequence.

Not the least curious part of the history of the act of 1828 is the treatment it has received from the protectionist writers.   At the time, the protectionists were far from enthusiastic about it.   Niles could not admit it to be a fair application of the protective policy,[1] while Matthew Carey called it a " crude mass of imperfection," and admitted it to be a disappointment to the protectionists.[2] In later years, however, when the details of history had been forgotten, it came to be regarded with more favor. The duties being on their face higher than those of previous years, it was considered a better application of protective principles. Henry C. Carey, on whose authority rest many of the accounts of our economic history, called it "an admirable tariff."[3] He represented it as having had great effect on the prosperity of the country, and his statements have often been repeated by protectionist writers.

It is almost impossible to trace the economic effect of any legislative measure that remains in force no more than four years ; and certainly we have not the materials for ascertaining the economic effects of the act of 1828. Taken by itself, that act is but a stray episode in our political history. It illustrates the change in the character of our public men and our public life which took place during the Jacksonian time. As an economic measure, it must be considered, not by itself, but as one of a series of

---

[1] Niles, XXXVII., 81 ; XXXVI., 113, and elsewhere. Niles objected especially to the $1.00 minimum on woollens.

[2] See his " Common-Sense Address " (1829), p. XI.; " The Olive Branch,'' No. III., p. 54 ; No. IV., p. 3 (1832).

[3] See his " Review of the Report of D. A. Wells " (1869), p. 4 ; and to the same effect, " Harmony of Interests," p. 5, and " Social Science," II., 225.

measures, begun tentatively in 1816, and carried out more vigorously in 1824, 1828, and 1832, by which a protective policy was maintained for some twenty years. It is very doubtful whether, with the defective information at our disposal, we can learn much as to the effect on the prosperity of the country even of the whole series of tariff acts. Probably we can reach conclusions of any value only on certain limited topics, such as the effects of protection to young industries during this time; as to the general effect of the protective measures we must rely on deduction from general principles. At all events, no one can trace the economic effects of the act of 1828. To ascribe to it the supposed prosperity of the years in which it was in in force, as Henry C. Carey and his followers have done, is only a part of that exaggeration of the effect of protective duties which is as common among their opponents as among their advocates.

THE TARIFF, 1830–1860.

In the years between 1832 and 1860 there was great vacillation in the tariff policy of the United States; there were also great fluctuations in the course of trade and industry. A low tariff was succeeded by a high tariff, which was in turn succeeded by another low tariff. Periods of undue inflation and of great demoralization, of prosperity and of depression, followed each other. The changes in the rates of duty and the fluctuations in industrial history have often been thought to be closely connected. Protectionists have ascribed prosperity to high tariffs, depression to low tariffs; free traders have reversed the inference. It is the object of the present essay to trace, so far as this can be done, the economic effect of tariff legislation during the thirty years of varying fortune that preceded the civil war.

First, by way of introduction, a sketch must be given of the history of the tariff. We begin with the tariff act of 1832, a distinctly protectionist measure, passed by the Whigs, or National Republicans, which put the protective system in a shape such as the advocates of protection hoped it might retain permanently. It levied high duties on cotton and woollen goods, iron, and other articles to which protection was meant to be applied. On articles not produced in the United States, either low duties were imposed, as on silks, or no duties at all, as on tea and coffee. The average rate on dutiable articles was about 33 per cent.

In 1833, the Compromise Tariff Act was passed, and remained in force until 1842. That act, there can be little doubt, was the result of an agreement between Clay and Calhoun, the leaders of the protectionists and free traders, while it secured also the support of the Jackson administration. Clay had been hitherto the most uncompromising of the protectionists; Calhoun had represented the extreme Southern demand that duties should be reduced to a horizontal level of 15 or 20 per cent.[1] The compromise provided for the retention of a considerable degree of protection for nearly nine years, and thereafter for a rapid reduction to a uniform 20 per cent. rate. The tariff of 1832 was the starting-point. All duties which in that tariff exceeded 20 per cent. were to have one tenth of the excess over 20 per cent. taken off on January 1, 1834; one tenth more on January 1, 1836; again one tenth in 1838; and another in 1840. That is, by 1840, four tenths of the excess over 20 per cent. would be gone.

---

[1] The Nullifiers had said that such a horizontal rate was the least they were willing to accept. See the Address to the People of the United States by the South Carolina Convention, in the volume of " State Papers on Nullification," published by the State of Massachusetts, p. 69.

Then, on January 1, 1842, one half the remaining excess was to be taken off ; and on July 1, 1842, the other half of the remaining excess was to go.   After July 1, 1842, therefore, there would be a uniform rate of 20 per cent. on all articles.   Obviously, the reduction was very gradual from 1833 till 1842, while in the first six months of 1842 a sharp and sudden reduction was to take place.

Considered as a political measure, the act of 1833 may deserve commendation.   As an economic or financial measure, there is little to be said for it.   It was badly drafted.   No provision was made in it as to specific duties; yet it was obviously meant to apply to such duties, and the Secretary of the Treasury had to take it on himself to frame rules as to the manner of ascertaining the *ad valorem* equivalents of specific duties and making the reductions called for by the act.[1]   Again, the reductions of duty were irregular.   Thus on one important article, rolled bar-iron, the duty of 1832 had been specific, —$1.50 per hundredweight.   This was equivalent, at the prices of 1832, to about 95 per cent.   The progress of the reductions is shown in the note.[2]   Up to 1842, they were

---

[1] The instructions issued from the Treasury Department may be found in "Exec. Doc." 1833-34, vol. I., No. 43.   It has been thought that the act did not apply to specific duties ; but this is a mistake.

[2]

Year.	Duty, per cent.
1834	87
1836	80
1838	72.5
1840	65
Jan. 1, 1842	42.5
July 5, 1842	20

This calculation is on the basis of the prices of 1833.   If prices changed

comparatively moderate ; but in the six months from January 1 to July 1, 1842, the duty dropped from 65 to 20 per cent. Producers and dealers necessarily found it hard to deal with such changes. It is true that a long warning was given them ; but, on the other hand, Congress might at any moment interfere to modify the act. Finally, and not least among the objections, there was the ultimate horizontal rate of 20 per cent.—a crude and indiscriminating method of dealing with the tariff problem, which can be defended on no ground of principle or expediency. The 20 per cent. rate, according to the terms of the act, was to remain in force indefinitely, that being the concession which in the end was made to the extremists of the South.[1]

As it happened, however, the 20 per cent. duty remained in force for but two months, from July 1 till September 1, 1842.[2] At the latter date the tariff act of 1842 went

(and they did change greatly), the rates under the Compromise Act would vary materially from those given in the text ; since the *ad valorem* equivalent of the specific duty, and its excess over 20 per cent., were ascertained for each year according to the prices of that year.

[1] Clay, who drafted the act, probably had no expectation that the 20 per cent. rate ever would go into effect. He thought Congress would amend before 1842, and intended to meet by his compromise the immediate emergency only. See his " Works," vol. II., pp. 131, 132. He tried to show Appleton and Davis, two leading representatives of the protectionists, that " no future Congress would be bound by the act." See Appleton's speech on the Tariff Act of 1842, " Appendix to Cong. Globe," 1841–42, p. 575.

[2] The Compromise Act was so loosely constructed that doubt was entertained whether under its terms any duties at all could be collected after June 30, 1842. The point was carried before the Supreme Court, which decided, however, that the rate of 20 per cent. was in effect during the two

into force. That act was passed by the Whigs as a party measure, and its history is closely connected with the political complications of the time. The Whigs had broken with President Tyler, and had a special quarrel with him as to the distribution among the States of the proceeds of the public lands. Tyler vetoed two successive tariff bills because of clauses in them in regard to distribution. The bill which he finally signed, and which became law, was passed hurriedly, without the distribution clause. Attention was turned mainly to the political quarrel and to the political effect of the bill in general.[1] The act, naturally enough, was a hasty and imperfect measure, of which the details had received little consideration. The duties which it levied were high,—probably higher than they would have been had the tariff discussion been less affected by the breach between Tyler and the Whigs. Though distinctively protective, and proclaimed to be such by the Whigs, it had not such a strong popular feeling behind it as had existed in favor of the protective measures of 1824, 1828, and 1832. In the farming States the enthusiasm for the home-market idea had cooled perceptibly; and in the manufacturing States the agitation came rather from the producers directly interested than

months before the act of 1842 went in force. (Aldridge *vs.* Williams, 3 Howard, 9.) Justice McLean dissented ; and there is much force to his dissenting opinion and to the argument of Reverdy Johnson, the counsel against the government.

[1] A full account of this struggle is in Von Holst's " Constitutional History," vol. III., pp. 451–463.

from the public at large. There is much truth in Calhoun's remark that the act of 1842 was passed, not so
much in compliance with the wishes of the manufacturers,
as because the politicians wanted an issue.[1]

The act of 1842 remained in force for but four years.
It was in turn superseded by the act of 1846, again a
political measure, passed this time by the Democrats.
The act of 1846 carried out the suggestions made by
Secretary Walker in his much debated Treasury Report
of 1845.   Indeed, it may be regarded as practically framed
by Walker, who professed to adhere to the principle of
free trade ; and the act of 1846 is often spoken of as an
instance of the application of free-trade principles.   In
fact, however, it effected no more than a moderation in
the application of protection.   The act established several
schedules, indicated by the letters A, B, C, D, and so on.
All the articles classed in schedule A paid 100 per cent.,
all in schedule B paid 40 per cent., all in schedule C paid
30 per cent., and so on for the rest.   Schedule C, with the
30 per cent. duty, included most articles with which the
protective controversy is concerned,—iron and metals in
general, manufactures of metals, wool and woollens, manufactures of leather, paper, glass, and wood.   Cottons
were in schedule D, and paid 25 per cent.   Tea and coffee,
on the other hand, were exempt from duty.

---

[1] " Works," vol. IV., pp. 199, 200.   Calhoun thought that a good deal
was due also to the influence of the " moneyed men " who wanted the
Treasury to be filled.

The act of 1846 remained in force till 1857, when a still further reduction of duties was made. The revenue was redundant in 1857, and this was the chief cause of the reduction of duties. The measure of that year was passed with little opposition, and was the first tariff act since 1816 that was not affected by politics.[1] It was agreed on all hands that a reduction of the revenue was imperatively called for, and, except from Pennsylvania, there was no opposition to the reduction of duties made in it. The framework of the act of 1846 was retained,—the schedules and the *ad valorem* duties. The duty on the important protective articles, in schedule C, was lowered to 24 per cent., cottons being transferred, moreover, to that schedule. Certain raw materials were at the same time admitted free of duty.

The act of 1857 remained in force till the close of the period we now have under examination. We begin with a high protective tariff in 1832 ; then follows a gradual reduction of duties, ending in 1842 with a brief period of very low duties. In the four years 1842–46 we have a strong application of protection. In 1846 begins what is often called a period of free trade, but is in reality one of moderated protection. In 1857 the protection is still further moderated, and for a few years there is as near an approach to free trade as the country has had since 1816.

---

[1] Seward said, in 1857, that "the vote of not a single Senator will be governed by any partisan consideration whatever." Appendix to "Congressional Globe," 1856–57, p. 344 ; and see Hunter's speech, *ibid.*, p. 331.

Turning now to the economic effect of this legislation, we have to note, first, its connection with the general prosperity of the country. That there was a distinct connection is asserted by both protectionists and free traders. The protectionists tell us that the compromise tariff caused the disastrous crises of 1837 and 1839; that the high tariff of 1842 brought back prosperity; that depression again followed the passage of the act of 1846, and that the panic of 1857 was precipitated by the tariff act of 1857. On the other hand, free traders not infrequently describe the period between 1846 and 1860 as one of exceptional prosperity, due to the low duties then in force.

It would not be worth while to allude to some of these assertions, if they were not so firmly imbedded in current literature and so constantly repeated in many accounts of our economic history. This is especially the case with the curious assertion that the crises of 1837 and 1839 were caused by the compromise tariff of 1833, or connected with it. This assertion had its origin in the writings of Henry C. Carey, who has been guilty of many curious versions of economic history, but of none more remarkable than this. It may be found in various passages in his works; and from them it has been transferred to the writings of his disciples and to the arguments of protectionist authors and speakers in general.[1] Yet no fair-

---

[1] References to the supposed effects of the act of 1833 abound in Carey's works. As good a specimen as any is this: "Agitation succeeded in producing a total change of system in the tariff of 1833. * * * Thencefor-

minded person, having even a superficial knowledge of the economic history of these years, can entertain such notions. The crises of 1837 and 1839 were obviously due to quite a different set of causes—to the bank troubles, the financial mistakes of Jackson's administration, the inflation of the currency, and to those general conditions of speculation and unduly expanded credit which give rise to crises. The tariff act had nothing whatever to do with them. Indeed, the reductions in duty under it, as we have

---

ward the building of furnaces and mills almost wholly ceased, the wealthy English capitalists having thus succeeded in regaining the desired control of the great American market for cloth and iron. As a consequence of their triumph there occurred a succession of crises of barbaric tendency, the whole terminating, in 1842, in a scene of ruin such as had never before been known, bankruptcy among the people being almost universal," etc. "Letters on the Iron Question" (1865), p. 4, printed in his "Miscellaneous Works" (1872). To the same effect, see his "Financial Crises," p. 18 ; "Review of Wells' Report," p. 5; "Social Science," II., p. 225. Professor Thompson makes the same statement in his "Political Economy," p. 353. See also Elder, "Questions of the Day" (1871), pp. 200, 201. Senator Evar's, in a speech made in 1883, ascribed to the act of 1833 "a bankruptcy which covered the whole land, without distinction of sections, with ruin." The pedigree of statements of this kind, which are frequent in campaign literature, can be traced back to Carey. Doubtless Carey wrote in good faith ; but his prejudices were so strong as to prevent him from taking a just view of economic history.

Oddly enough, Calhoun ascribed the crisis of 1837 to the fact that duties under the act of 1833 remained *too high*. The high duties brought in a large revenue and caused a surplus in the Treasury ; the deposit and distribution of this brought inflation and speculation, and eventually a crisis ("Works," IV., p. 174). No doubt the high duties were one cause of the government surplus, and thereby aided in bringing about the crisis, so that this view, incomplete as it is, has more foundation than Carey's explanation. On the other hand, Clay, as might be expected, took pains to deny that the act of 1833 had any thing to do with the troubles of the years following its passage ("Works," II., pp. 530, 531 ; edition of 1844).

seen, were slight until 1840, and could hardly have influenced in any degree the breaking out of the panics. Even if the reductions of duty had been greater, and had been made earlier, they would probably have had no effect, favorable or unfavorable, on the inflation of the earlier years or on the depression which followed.

We may dispose at this point of a similar assertion occasionally made in regard to the crisis of 1857,—that the tariff act of 1857 caused or intensified it. This view also is traceable, probably, to Carey. It appears in his writings and in those of his disciples.[1] In fact, the crisis of 1857 was an unusually simple case of activity, speculation, over-banking, panic, and depression; and it requires the exercise of great ingenuity to connect it in any way with the tariff act. As it happened, indeed, the tariff was passed with some hope that it would serve to prevent the crisis. Money was accumulating in the Treasury; and it was hoped that by reducing duties the revenue would be diminished, money would be got out of the Treasury, and the stringency, which was already threatening, prevented.[2]

---

[1] Carey speaks in one place of " the terrific free-trade crisis of 1857." " Letters to Colfax," p. 15 ; " Financial Crises," p. 8 ; " Review of Wells," p. 5 (all in his " Miscellaneous Works "). Thompson (" Political Economy," p. 357) says : " In 1857, Congress reduced the duties twenty-five per cent. * * * It at once intensified all the unwholesome tendencies in our commercial and industrial life. * * * Another great panic followed through the collapse of unsound enterprises."

[2] See a letter from a Boston merchant to Senator Wilson, "Congr. Globe, 1856–57, Appendix," p. 344 ; and the statement by Senator Hunter, *ibid.*, 329.

The reduction failed to prevent the panic; but, at the time, it would have been considered very odd to ascribe the disaster to the tariff act.

On the other hand, it has been very often said that the activity of trade in 1843–44 was due to the enactment of the protective tariff act of 1842. There may be a degree of truth in this. The unsettled state of legislation on the tariff before the act of 1842 was passed must have been an obstacle to the revival of confidence. After July 1, 1842, there was the uniform duty of 20 per cent.; nay, it was doubtful whether there was by law even that duty in force. It was certain that Congress would wish not to retain the horizontal rate, but would try to enact a new tariff law; yet the quarrel between the Whigs and Tyler made the issue quite doubtful. Such uncertainty necessarily operated as a damper on trade; and the passage of any act whatever, settling the tariff question for the time being, would have removed one great obstacle to the return of activity and prosperity. It is even possible that the passage of the act of 1842 may have had a more direct effect than this. No doubt, in the regular recurrence of waves of activity and depression, the depression of 1840–42 would soon have been followed, in any event, by a period of activity. The point at which activity will begin to show itself under such circumstances is largely a matter of chance. It begins, for some perhaps accidental reason, with one industry or set of idustries, and, the materials for general revival being ready, then spreads quickly to the others.   In the same way, when the materials for a crisis are at hand, a single accidental failure may precipitate a general panic.   In 1842–43 the high duties of the tariff act probably helped to make profits large for the time being in certain manufactures, notably those of cotton and iron.   Prosperity in these set in, and may have been the signal for a general revival of confidence and for a general extension of business operations. To that extent, it is not impossible that the protective tariff of 1842 was the occasion of the reviving business of the ensuing years.   But it is a very different thing from this to say that the tariff was the cause of prosperity, and that depression would have continued indefinitely but for the re-establishment of high protective duties.

In truth, there has been a great deal of loose talk about tariffs and crises.   Whenever there has been a crisis, the free traders or protectionists, as the case may be, have been tempted to use it as a means for overthrowing the system they opposed.   Cobden found in the depression of 1839–40 a powerful argument in his crusade against the corn laws, and knew that a return of prosperity would work against him.[1]   Within a few years, the opponents of protection in this country have found in general depression a convenient and effective argument against the tariff.   In the same way, the protectionists have been tempted to use the crises of 1837 and 1857, and conversely

---

[1] See passages in Morley's " Life of Cobden," pp. 162, 163, 210.

the revival of 1843–44, to help their case. But the effect of tariffs cannot be traced by any such rough-and-ready method. The tariff system of a country is but one of many factors entering into its general prosperity. Its influence, good or bad, may be strengthened or may be counteracted by other causes; while it is exceedingly difficult, generally impossible, to trace its separate effect. Least of all can its influence be traced in those variations of outward prosperity and depression which are marked by " good times " and crises. A protective tariff may sometimes strengthen other causes which are bringing on a commercial crisis. Some such effect is very likely traceable to the tariff in the years before the crisis of 1873. It may sometimes be the occasion of a revival of activity, when the other conditions are already favorable to such a revival. That may have been the case in 1843. But these are only incidental effects, and lie quite outside the real problem as to the results of protection. As a rule, the tariff system of a country operates neither to cause nor to prevent crises. They are the results of conditions of exchange and production on which it can exercise no great or permanent influence.

Remarks of the same kind may be made on the frequent assertion that the prosperity of the country from 1846 to 1860 can be traced to the low duties then in force. He who is convinced, on grounds of general reasoning and of general experience, that the principles of

free trade are sound and that protective duties are harmful, can fairly deduce the conclusion that the low tariffs
of 1846 and 1857 contributed, so far as they went, to general prosperity.   But a direct connection cannot be traced.
A number of favorable causes were at work, such as the
general advance in the arts, the rapid growth of the rail-
way system and of ocean communication, the Californian
gold discoveries.   There is no way of eliminating the
other factors, and determining how much can be ascribed
to the tariff alone.   Even in the growth of international
trade, where some direct point of connection might be
found, we cannot measure the effect of low duties; for
international trade was growing between all countries
under the influence of cheapened transportation and the
stimulus of the great gold discoveries.[1]   The inductive,
or historical, method absolutely fails us here.

---

[1] The growth of foreign trade under the tariffs of 1846 and 1857 was certainly very striking.   In Grosvenor's " Does Protection Protect ? " there is
a table showing the imports and exports per head of population from 1821
to 1869, in which it is stated that the annual average per head of population was :

	Imports.	Exports.
In 1843–46,	$4.66	$5.22
" 1847–50,	6.35	6.32
" 1851–55,	9.10	7.35
" 1856–60,	10.41	9.45

The imports and exports were, in millions of dollars :

	Imports.	Exports.
Annual average of the four years 1843–46,	92.7	100
" " " " " " 1847–50,	138.3	136.8
" " " " five " 1851–55,	231.	186.2
" " " " " " 1856–60,	305.	278.2

But how are we to measure the share which low duties had in promoting
this growth ?

We turn now to another inquiry, as to the effect of the fluctuating duties of this period on the protected industries. That inquiry, it is hardly necessary to say, leads us to no certain conclusion as to the effect of the duties on the welfare of the country at large. It is quite conceivable, and indeed on grounds of general reasoning at least probable, that any stimulus given to the protected industries indicated a loss in the productive powers of the community as a whole. But it has often been asserted, and again often denied, that the duties caused a growth of certain industries; and it is worth while to trace, if we can, the tangible effect in this direction, even though it be but a part of the total effect.

It is the production of iron in the unmanufactured form that has been most hotly discussed in the protective controversy. And in regard to this, fortunately, we have good, if not complete, information.

The duty on pig-iron had been 62½ cents a hundredweight under the tariff act of 1828. In 1832 it was reduced to 50 cents, or $10 per ton. This rate was equivalent to about 40 per cent. on the foreign price at that time; and, under the Compromise Act of 1833, it was gradually reduced, until it reached 20 per cent. in 1842. Under the act of 1842, the duty was again raised to $10 a ton. In 1846 it was made 30 per cent. on the value, and in 1857 24 per cent. As the value varied, the duty under the last two acts varied also. In 1847, a time of high prices, the duty of 30 per cent. was equal to $5.75 per ton; in 1852 it was only $3.05; in 1855 it was as high as $6; in 1860 it again fell to $3.40.[1]

The duty on bar-iron was of two kinds until 1846,—a duty on hammered bar-iron, and another heavier duty on rolled bar-iron. The duty on hammered bar was, in 1832, fixed at 90 cents per hundredweight, or $18 per ton. That on rolled bar was nearly twice as heavy, being $30 per ton, or nearly 100 per cent. on the value. These duties were reduced under the Compromise Act; and, as we have seen, the reduction on rolled bar was very great, and, in 1842, very sudden. Under the act of 1842, the duty on hammered bar was made $17 per ton, that on rolled bar $25 per ton. The act of 1846 gave up finally the discrimination between the two kinds, and admitted

---

[1] The duty from year to year, on the average, for the fiscal years ending June 30th, is given in the following table. The foreign value, on which the duty was computed, is also given. The figures are compiled from the tables given in French, " History of Iron Manufacture," p. 70, and in the " Report of the Iron and Steel Association for 1876," p. 182.

Year ending June 30th.	Average value.	Duty (30 per cent. till 1857, 24 per cent. after 1857.)
1847	$19.90	$5.95
1848	15.80	4.75
1849	13.30	4.00
1850	12.70	3.80
1851	12.60	3.75
1852	10.20	3.05
1853	13.40	4.00
1854	18.00	5.40
1855	20.00	6.00
1856	19.80	5 95
1857	19.50	5.85
1858	17.60	4.20
1859	15.20	3.65
1860	14.10	3.40

both alike at a duty of 30 per cent.; and the act of 1857 admitted them at 24 per cent.[1]

Before proceeding to examine the economic effect of these duties, it should be said that our information as to the production of iron is in many ways defective, and that the statements relating to it in the following paragraphs cannot be taken to be more than roughly accurate. The government figures give us trustworthy information as to the imports; but for the domestic production we must rely, at least for the earlier years, on estimates which are often no more than guesses. Nevertheless, the general trend of events can be made out pretty clearly, and we are able to draw some important conclusions.[2]

It seems to be clear that the importation of iron was somewhat affected by the duties. The years before 1842, when the compromise tariff was in force, were years of such disturbance that it is not easy to trace any effects clearly to the operation of the tariff; but imports during these years were a smaller proportion of the total consumption of iron than they were during the period after

---

[1] Between 1832 and 1842, an exception had been made for one class of rolled iron,—iron rails actually laid down on railroads. These were admitted free of duty; or, rather, a drawback was granted of the full amount of duty due or paid on them. Between 1828 and 1832, a drawback had been granted such as to make the duty on railroad iron only 25 per cent. After 1842, however, it was charged with duty like any other iron.

[2] The reader who wishes to examine further the data as to the production of iron before 1860, is referred to the Appendix to the *Quarterly Journal of Economics* for April, 1888, vol. II., pp. 377–382, where I have considered the figures in detail.

1846. It must be remembered that from 1830 till 1842 all railroad iron was admitted free of duty, and that a large part of the imported iron consisted of rails. If this quantity be deducted from the total import, the remaining quantity, which alone was affected by the duties, becomes still smaller as compared with the domestic product. In 1841 and 1842, when duties began to be low under the operation of the Compromise Act, imports were larger in proportion to the home product. On the other hand, in the four years, 1843–46, under the act of 1842, they show a distinct decrease. After 1847, they show as distinct an increase, and continue to be large throughout the period until 1860. In the speculative and railroad-building years, from 1852 to 1857, the importation was especially heavy; and in 1853 and 1854 the total quantity of iron imported was almost as great as the home product.

The most effective part of the iron duties until 1846 was the heavy discriminating duty on rolled bar-iron. That duty amounted (from 1818 till 1846, except during a few months in 1842) to about 100 per cent. Rolled iron, made by the puddling process and by rolling, is the form of bar-iron now in common use. The process was first applied successfully by Cort in England about 1785, and in that country was immediately put into extensive use. It made bar-iron much more cheaply and plentifully than the old process of refining in a forge and under a hammer; and, at the present time, hammered bar of the old-fashioned kind has ceased to be made, except in comparatively small quantities for special purposes. Cort's processes of puddling and rolling were practicable only through the use of bituminous coal and coke. The abundant and excellent coal of Great Britain gave that country an enormous advantage in producing rolled iron, as it had already done in smelting pig-iron, and put her in that commanding position as an iron producer which she continues to occupy to the present day. When rolled iron first began to be exported from England to foreign countries, it aroused strong feelings of jealousy, being so much cheaper than other iron. Several countries fought against the improvement by imposing discriminating duties on it.[1] That course was adopted in the United States. In 1818, a discriminating duty was put on rolled iron, partly because it was said to be inferior in quality to hammered iron, and partly from a feeling in favor of protecting the domestic producers of hammered iron. The duty was retained, as we have seen, till 1846. Its effect was neutralized in part by the free admission of railroad iron, which was one form of rolled iron; but, so far as it was applied to rolled iron in general, it simply prevented the United States from sharing the benefit of a great improvement in the arts. It had no effect in hastening the use of the puddling and rolling processes in the country. Though introduced into the United States as early as

---

[1] In France a discriminating duty equivalent to 120 per cent. was imposed in 1833 on iron imported by sea, *i. e.*, on English iron. Armé, "Tarifs de Douanes," I., 144, 145. The discrimination was maintained until 1855. *Ibid.*, 271.

1817, these processes got no firm hold until after anthracite coal began to be used, about 1840, as an iron-making fuel.[1]

We turn now to the history of the domestic production. By far the most important event in that history is the use of anthracite coal as a fuel, which began about 1840. The substitution of anthracite for wood (charcoal) revolutionized the iron trade in the United States in the same way as the use of bituminous coal (coke) had revolution-

---

[1] The first puddling and rolling mill in the United States was put up in Pennsylvania in 1817. The first puddling in New England was done as late as 1835. Wood was used as fuel at the outset. Swank, "Iron in All Ages," 166, 330. The effect of the duty on rolled iron cannot be better described than in the clear and forcible language used by Gallatin in 1831 : "It seems impracticable that iron made with charcoal can ever compete with iron made from bituminous coal. * * * A happy application of anthracite coal to the manufacture of iron, the discovery of new beds of bituminous coal, the erection of iron-works in the vicinity of the most Easterly beds now existing, and the improved means of transportation, which may bring this at a reasonable rate to the sea-border, may hereafter enable the American iron-master to compete in cheapness with foreign rolled iron in the Atlantic districts. On those contingencies the tariff can have no effect. To persist, in the present state of the manufacture, in that particular competition, and for that purpose to proscribe the foreign rolled iron, is to compel the people for an indefinite time to substitute a dear for a cheap article. It is said that the British iron is generally of inferior quality ; this is equally true of a portion of that made in America. In both cases the consumer is the best judge,—has an undoubted right to judge for himself. Domestic charcoal iron should confine itself to a competition with the foreign iron made from the same fuel." Gallatin added, prophetically : "Your memorialists believe that the ultimate reduction of the price of American iron to that of British rolled iron can only, and ultimately will, be accomplished in that Western region which abounds with ore, and in which are found the most extensive formations of bituminous coal."— "Memorial of the Free-Trade Convention," pp. 60, 61.

ized the English iron trade nearly a century before. Up to 1840, pig-iron had been smelted in this country with charcoal, a fuel which was expensive, and tended to become more and more expensive as the nearer forests were cut down and wood became less easily attainable. Charcoal pig-iron could not have competed on even terms with the coal-made English iron. But between 1830 and 1840 it was protected by the heavy duties on English iron ; and, under their shelter, the production in those years steadily increased. There seems to be no doubt that, with lower duties or no duties at all, the domestic production would have been less, and the import greater. In other words, the duty operated as a true protective duty, hampering international trade and increasing the price of the home product as well as of the imported iron.

In 1840, however, anthracite coal began to be applied to the making of pig-iron. The use of anthracite was made possible by the hot blast,—a process which was put in successful operation in England at nearly the same time.[1] The importance of the new method was immediately appreciated, and predictions were made that henceforth there would be no longer occasion for importing iron, even under the 20 per cent. duty of the Compromise Act. Many furnaces were changed from the charcoal to the

---

[1] The hot blast was successfully applied in a furnace in Pennsylvania in 1835, but the experiment was not prosecuted. In 1837, Crane applied it in Wales, and about the same time the process was successfully used in this country. Swank, " Iron in All Ages," 268–273 ; French, " History of the Iron Trade," 58–60.

anthracite method.[1] At very nearly the same time, as it happened, the tariff act of 1842 was passed, imposing heavy duties on all kinds of iron, among others on the railroad iron which had hitherto been admitted free. Very shortly afterwards a general revival of trade set in. Under the influence of these combined causes, the production of iron was suddenly increased. The exact amount of the increase is disputed; but the production seems to have risen from somewhere near 300,000 tons in 1840–41, to 650,000 or more in 1846–47. Some part of this great growth was certainly due to the high protection of 1842 ; but, under any circumstances, the use of anthracite would have given a great stimulus to the iron trade. This is shown by the course of events under the tariff acts of 1846 and 1857. The production remained, on the whole, fairly steady throughout the years when these acts were in force. There was, on the whole, an increase from between 500,000 and 600,000 tons in the earlier years of the period to between 800,000 and 900,000 tons in the later years. For a few years after the passage of the act of 1846, the reduction of the duty to 30 per cent. had little, if any, effect. Prices were high both in England and in the United States ; for it was a time of active railroad building in England, and consequently of great demand for iron. The *ad valorem* duty was correspond-

---

[1] See the notices in Hazard's "Statistical Register," I., pp. 335, 363 ; III., p. 173 ; IV., p. 207. That great results were at once expected from the new method is shown by an interesting speech of Nicholas Biddle's, *ibid.*, II., p. 230.

ingly high. In 1850–51 the usual reaction set in, prices went down, production decreased, and the iron-masters complained.[1] But the natural revival came after a year or two. Prices rose again ; production increased, and continued to increase until 1860. Although the duty, which had been $9 a ton under the act of 1842, was no more than $3 and $4 under the 24 per cent. rate which was in force during the years 1858, 1859, and 1860, and although these were not years of unusual general activity, the domestic production showed a steady growth. The country was growing fast, many railroads were in course of construction, much iron was needed. An undiminished home product was consumed, as well as largely increased imports.

The most significant fact in the iron trade, however, is to be seen, not in the figures of total production, but in the shifting from charcoal to anthracite iron. While the total product remained about the same, the component elements changed greatly. The production of anthracite

---

[1] The iron-masters admitted that the act of 1846 had been sufficiently protective when first passed. But in 1849 and 1850, they began to complain and ask for higher duties. See " Proceedings of Iron Convention at Pittsburg (1849)," p. 9 ; " Proceedings of Convention at Albany," pp. 27, 42. They certainly had a legitimate subject for complaint in the operation of the *ad valorem* duty, in that it tended to exaggerate the fluctuations of prices. When prices abroad were high, the duty was high ; when prices abroad were low, the duty was low. Consequently, the price of foreign iron in the United States, which is the sum of the foreign price and the duty, fluctuated more widely than the foreign price alone. This was certainly an evil, especially with an article whose price was liable under any conditions to vary so much as the price of iron. See the table above, p. 124.

iron rose steadily: that of charcoal iron fell as steadily. The first anthracite furnace was built in 1840. In 1844 there were said to be twenty furnaces, making 65,000 tons annually.[1] Thence the production rose with hardly an interruption being

in 1844	.	.	.	.	65,000 gross tons.
" 1846	.	.	.	.	110,000 " "
" 1849	.	.	.	.	115,000 " "
" 1854	.	.	.	.	308,000 net "
" 1855	.	.	.	.	343,000 " "
" 1856	.	.	.	.	394,000 " "

As the anthracite iron production increased, that of charcoal iron decreased. Under the tariff act of 1842, a large number of new charcoal furnaces had been put up.[2] Many of these had to be given up under the combined competition of anthracite and of English iron. Some maintained themselves by using coke and raw bituminous coal, in those parts of the country where bituminous coal was to be had[4]; others disappeared. That at least some

[1] See a " Letter of the Philadelphia Coal and Iron Trade to the Committee on Finance " (pamphlet. Philadelphia, 1844).

[2] The figure for 1846 is that given in Taylor, " Statistics of Coal," p. 133. Swank gives the figure for 1846 as 123,000 (gross ?) tons. " Iron in All Ages," p. 274. The figures for 1849–56 are from Lesley, " Iron Manufacturers' Guide (1859)," pp. 751,752. Those given by Grosvenor, " Does Protection Protect ? " p. 225, vary somewhat ; but the differences are not great.

[3] See the figures in Grosvenor, p. 215. There were built in 1843 9 charcoal furnaces ; in 1844, 23 ; in 1845, 35 ; in 1846, 44 ; in 1847, 34 ; in 1848, 28 ; in 1849, 14.

[4] The use of coke began in the United States about 1850, but was of little importance until after 1856. The use of raw bituminous coal was introduced about 1850 in the Shenango and Mahoning valleys (on the border

of them should disappear was inevitable. Charcoal iron for general use was a thing of the past ; and the effect of the tariff of 1842 was to call into existence a number of furnaces which used antiquated methods, and before long must have been displaced in any event by anthracite furnaces

The use of anthracite not only stimulated the production of pig-iron, but also that of rolled iron and railroad bars. Anthracite was first used in puddling and reheating in 1844 and 1845,[1] and thenceforward rolled iron was made regularly in large quantities. In 1856 the production of rolled iron was nearly 500,000 tons.[2] Iron rails first began to be made while the tariff act of 1842 was in force, though the steps towards making them were taken even before that act put an end to the free admission of English rails.[3] With the decline in railroad building and the

---

between Pennsylvania and Ohio), where there is suitable coal. Swank, " Iron in All Ages," pp. 281–284. In the " Report of the American Iron and Steel Association for 1876 " (prepared by Swank), the following figures are given of the production of iron with the various kinds of fuel. I have selected a few typical years :

Year.	Anthracite iron.	Charcoal iron.	Bituminous coal and coke iron.	Total.
1854	339,000	342,000	55,000	736,000
1856	443,000	370,000	70,000	883,000
1858	362,000	285,000	58,000	705,000
1860	519,000	278,000	122,000	919,000

The figures here denote net tons.

[1] Speech of A. S. Hewitt, in " Proceedings of Iron Convention at Albany " (1849), p. 54.

[2] Lesley, " Iron Manufacturers' Guide," p. 761.

[3] See a pamphlet, " Observations on the Expediency of Repealing the Act by which Railroad Iron is Released from Duty," 1842. It gives an account of large rolling mills then being erected at Danville, Pennsylvania.

general fall in iron prices, which took place in 1849, many of the rail mills stopped work.   But the business revived with the general prosperity which set in early in the decade, and the production of rails steadily increased until 1856.   Under the influence of the crisis of 1857 it fell, but soon rose again, and in 1860 was more than 200,000 tons.[1]

To sum up: The high duty on iron in its various forms between 1832 and 1841, and again in 1842–46, impeded importation, retarded for the United States that cheapening of iron which has been one of the most important factors in the march of improvement in this century, and maintained in existence costly charcoal furnaces long after that method had ceased in Great Britain to be in general use.   The first step towards a vigorous and healthy growth of the iron industry was in the use of anthracite in 1840.   That step, so far from being promoted by the high duties, was taken in a time when duties were on the point of being reduced to the 20 per cent. level. Hardly had it been taken when the high duties of the tariff act of 1842 brought about (not indeed alone, but in conjunction with other causes) a temporary return to the

---

[1] See the figures given in "Report of Iron and Steel Association for 1876," p. 165.   The production of rails is there stated to have been :

In 1849	.	.	.	.	.	.	24,000 tons.
" 1850	.	.	.	.	.	.	44,000 "
" 1854	.	.	.	.	.	.	108,000 "
" 1856	.	.	.	.	.	.	180,000 "
" 1857	.	.	.	.	.	.	162,000 "
" 1860	.	.	.	.	.	.	205,000 "

old charcoal process. A number of new charcoal furnaces were built, unsuited to the industry of the time and certain to succumb before long. Under the lower duties from 1846 to 1860, the charcoal production gradually became a less and less important part of the iron industry, and before the end of the period had been restricted to those limits within which it could find a permanent market for the special qualities of its iron.[1] On the other hand, the lower duties did not prevent a steady growth in the making of anthracite iron; while the production of railroad iron and of rolled iron in general, also made possible by the use of anthracite, showed a similar steady progress. There is no reason to doubt that, had there been no duty at all, there would yet have been a large production of anthracite pig- and rolled iron. Meanwhile the country was rapidly developing, and needed much iron. The low duties permitted a large importation of foreign iron, in addition to a large domestic production. The comparative cheapness and abundance of so important an industrial agent could not have operated otherwise than to promote material prosperity.

We turn now to another industry,—the manufacture of cotton goods, by far the largest and most important branch of the textile industry. Here we are met at the

---

[1] Charcoal iron has qualities which cause a certain quantity of it to be in demand under any circumstances. Since it settled down, about 1860, to its normal place as a supplement to coal-made iron, the product has steadily increased with the growing needs of the country. In the years 1863–65 the annual product was about 240,000 tons. In 1886 it was 460,000 tons.

outset by the fact that, at the beginning of the period which we are considering, the cotton manufacture was in the main independent of protection, and not likely to be much affected, favorably or unfavorably, by changes in duties. Probably as early as 1824, and almost certainly by 1832, the industry had reached a firm position, in which it was able to meet foreign competition on equal terms.[1] Mr. Nathan Appleton, who was a large owner of cotton factory stocks, and who was also, in his time, one of the ablest and most prominent advocates of protective duties, said in 1833 that at that date coarse cottons could not have been imported from England if there had been no duty at all, and that even on many grades of finer goods competition was little to be feared. In regard to prints, the American goods were, quality for quality, as cheap as the English, but might be supplanted, in the absence of duties, by the poorer and nominally cheaper English goods,—an argument, often heard in our own day, which obviously puts the protective system on the ground of regulating the quality of goods for consumers. The general situation of the cotton manufacture, as described by Appleton, was one in which duties had ceased to be a factor of much importance in its development.[2]

---

[1] See the previous essay on " Protection to Young Industries," Part III., where an account is given of the history of the cotton manufacture up to 1824.

[2] See Appleton's speech on the Verplanck bill of 1833, " Congressional Debates," IX., pp. 1216–1217. Compare his remarks in the same volume at p. 1579.

During the extraordinary fluctuations of industry and the gradual reduction of duties which ensued under the compromise tariff of 1833, the business of manufacturing cottons was profitable and expanded, or encountered depression and loss, in sympathy with the industry of the country at large, being influenced chiefly by the expansion of credit and the rise of prices before 1837 and 1839, and the crisis and liquidation that followed those years. Notwithstanding the impending reductions of duty under the Compromise Act, large investments were made in the business in the earlier part of the period. Thus, in 1835–36, the Amoskeag Company began on a large scale its operations in Manchester, N. H.[1] The depression at the close of the decade checked growth for a while, but did not prevent new investments from being made, even before the passage of the act of 1842 settled the tariff uncertainty.[2] The best informed judges said that the causes of increase or decrease of profit had been, as one might expect, the same as those that produced fluctuations in other branches of business; and they made no mention of duties or of tariff.[3] Appleton's account of the

[1] Potter, "History of Manchester," p. 552. The Stark Mills were built in 1838, the second Stark Mills in 1839.

[2] Earl, "History of Fall River," pp. 35–37. "From the panic of 1837, which affected every business centre in the country, Fall River seems to have speedily recovered, since within a few years from that date nearly every mill in the place was enlarged, though only one new one was built." *Ibid.*, p. 53.

[3] See the answers from T. G. Cary, treasurer of a Lowell mill, and from Samuel Batchelder to circulars sent out in 1845 by Secretary Walker. Batch-

stage reached by the industry finds confirmation in a careful volume on the cotton manufacture in the United
States, published in 1840 by Robert Montgomery. This
writer's general conclusions are much the same as those
which competent observers reach for our own time.
Money wages were about twice as high in the United
States, but the product per spindle and per loom was
considerably greater. The cotton, in his time, was not so
well mixed, not so thoroughly cleaned, not so well carded
in the United States as in England ; but, on the other
hand, the Americans were superior in ordinary power-loom
weaving, as well as in warping and dressing. Elaborate
tables are given of the expenses per unit of product in
both countries, the final result of which, when all things
were considered, showed a difference of three per cent. in
favor of the American manufactures. Calculations of
this kind, which are common enough in discussions of
protective duties, are apt to express inadequately the
multiplicity of circumstances which affect concrete industry ; yet they may gauge with fair accuracy the general
conditions, and in this case were made intelligently and
without bias. It is worth noting that Montgomery attrib-
utes the success of the Americans in exporting cottons to

elder, our most trustworthy informant on the early history of the cotton
manufacture, writes that " the increase and decrease of profit from 1831 to
1844 have conformed very nearly to the general prosperity of the country."
The circulars and answers are printed in the appendices to Walker's Report.   Exec. Doc. 1845–46, vol. II., No. 6, pp. 215, 216, 313.

greater honesty in manufacturing and to the superior quality of their goods.[1]

During the years following the passage of the act of 1842, by which the duties on cottons were increased largely, the manufacturers made high profits. In Secretary Walker's Report, and in other attacks on protective duties, much was made of this circumstance, the high profits being ascribed to the new duties. The protectionists denied the connection, and a lively controversy ensued.[2] The truth seems to be that the case was not different from that usually presented in economic phenomena,—several causes combined to produce a single general effect. The high duties very likely served, in part, to enable a general advance of profits to be maintained for several years. But there was also an increased

---

[1] See "Montgomery's "Cotton Manufacture," pp. 29, 38, 82, 86, 91, 101. The tables of expenses are on pp. 124, 125 ; the remarks on quality of goods, on pp. 130, 194 ; on wages and product, on pp. 118–121, 123. Montgomery was superintendent of the York Factories at Saco, Maine, of which Samuel Batchelder was treasurer. Allusions to Montgomery's book, and confirmation of some of his conclusions, may be found in Batchelder's " Early Progress of the Cotton Manufacture," p. 80 and following.

At a convention in favor of protection, held in New York in 1842, committees were appointed on various industries. The committee on cottons reported a recommendation to Congress of minimum duties on plain and printed goods, but added that these duties were " more than is necessary for much the largest part of the cotton goods," and that " most of the printed calicoes are now offered to the consumer at lower prices than they could be imported under a tariff for revenue only."

[2] See T. G. Cary, " Results of Manufactures at Lowell," Boston, 1845 ; N. Appleton, " Review of Secretary Walker's Report," 1846 ; and the speeches of Rockwell, "Congr. Globe," 1845–46, pp. 1034–1037, and Winthrop, *ibid.*, Appendix, p. 969.

export to China, which proved highly profitable. More-over, the price of raw cotton was low in these years, lag-ging behind the advance in the prices of cotton goods; and, as long as this lasted, the manufacturers made large gains. The fact that prosperity was shared by the cotton manufacturers in England shows that other causes than the new tariff must have been at work.

On the other hand, when the act of 1846 was passed, the protectionists predicted disaster [1]; but disaster came not, either for the country at large or for the cotton in-dustry. Throughout the period from 1846 to 1860 the manufacture of cotton grew steadily, affected by the gen-eral conditions of trade, but little influenced by the lower duties. Exact figures indicating its fortunes are not to be had, yet we have enough information to enable us to judge of the general trend of events. The number of spindles in use gives the best indication of the growth of cotton manufacturing. We have no trustworthy figures as to the number of spindles in the whole country; but we have figures, collected by a competent and well-informed writer, in regard to Massachusetts. That State has always been the chief seat of the cotton manufacture, and its progress there doubtless indicates what took place in the country at large. The number of spindles in Massachu-

---

[1] Abbott Lawrence predicted in 1849 that " all this [a general crash] will take place in the space of eighteen months from the time this experimental bill goes into operation ; not a specie-paying bank doing business will be found in the United States." " Letters to Rives," p. 12. Appleton made a similar prediction in his " Review of Walker's Report," p. 28.

setts, which was, in round numbers, 340,000 in 1831, had nearly doubled in 1840, was over 800,000 in 1845, and was over 1,600,000 in 1860, having again nearly doubled during the period of low duties.[1] The same signs of growth and prosperity are seen in the figures of the consumption of raw cotton in the United States, which, compiled independently, reach the same general result. Between the first half of the decade 1840-50, and the second half of the decade 1850–60, the quantity of raw cotton used in the mills of the United States about doubled. The annual consumption, which had been about 150,000 bales in 1830, rose to an average of more than 300,000 bales in the early years of the next decade, and again to one of more than 600,000 bales in the years 1850-54. In the five years immediately preceding the civil war, the average annual consumption was about

---

[1] The following figures are given by Samuel Batchelder in a " Report to the Boston Board of Trade," made in 1860 (published separately ; the essential parts printed also in " Hunt's Merchants' Magazine," xlv., p. 14) :

Spindles in Massachusetts :

In 1831	.	.	.	340,000
" 1840	.	.	.	624,500 (other sources make it 665,000).
" 1845	.	.	.	817,500
" 1850	.	.	.	1,288,000
" 1855	.	.	.	1,519,500
" 1860	.	.	.	1,688,500

For New England, and the United States as a whole, Batchelder gives the following figures, taken from De Bow, for the years 1840 and 1850. They are not entirely trustworthy, but may be accepted as roughly accurate. We add the census figures for 1860 :

Spindles in

			New England.			United States.
1840	.	.	1,597,000	.	.	2,112,000
1850	.	.	2,751,000	.	.	3,634,000
1860	,	,	3,859,000	.	.	5,236,000

800,000 bales. During these years the consumption of cotton in Great Britain seems to have increased at very nearly the same rate.[1] Such figures indicate that the cotton manufacture was advancing rapidly and steadily. Another sign of its firm position is the steady increase during the same period in the exports of cotton goods, chiefly to China and the East. The value of the cotton goods exported averaged but little over $3,000,000 annually between 1838 and 1843, rose to over $4,000,000 between 1844 and 1849, was nearly $7,000,000 a year between 1851 and 1856, was over $8,000,000 in 1859, and almost touched $11,000,000 in 1860. An industry which regularly exports a large part of its products can hardly be stimulated to any considerable extent by protective duties. No doubt, the absence of high duties had an effect on the range of the industry. It was confined mainly to the production of plain, cheap, staple cotton cloths, and was not extended to the making of finer and " fancy " goods. But, even under the high protective duties of the last twenty-five years, the bulk of the product has continued to be of the first mentioned kind, and cottons of that grade have been sold, quality for quality, at prices not above those of foreign goods; while comparatively little progress has been made in the manufacture of the finer grades.[2]

---

[1] The reader is referred to the Appendix to the *Quarterly Journal of Economics* for April, 1888, for tables of the consumption of cotton and of the exports of cotton goods.

[2] Batchelder, who was a decided advocate of proctection, wrote in 1861 a

The situation of the woollen manufacture differs in some important respects from that of the cotton manufacture, most noticeably in that it is less favorable as regards the supply of raw material. The maker of cotton goods is sure of securing at home cotton of the best quality at a price below that which his foreign rival must pay. But many qualities of wool cannot be produced to advantage in the United States; while others cannot be grown at all, or at least, notwithstanding very heavy protective duties, never have been grown. Moreover, the raw material, when obtained, is neither so uniform in quality nor so well adapted to treatment by machinery as is the fibre of cotton. Wool is of the most diverse quality, varying from a fine silk-like fibre to a

---

series of articles for the Boston *Commercial Advertiser*, in which, after comparing the prices and qualities of English and American shirtings, he said : " The inquiry may then be made, What occasion is there for a protective duty ? The answer is : There would be none in the ordinary course of business. But there are sometimes occasions when * * * there has been a great accumulation of goods in the hands of manufacturers abroad, so that, if crowded on their market, it would depress the price of the usual supply of their customers at home. On such occasions, our warehouse system affords the opportunity, at little expense, to send the goods here, where they may be ready to be thrown on the market to be sold," etc.

In Ellison's " Handbook of the Cotton Trade," it is stated, at p. 29 ; " It is believed that, had it not been for the free-trade policy of Great Britain, the manufacturing system of America would at the present time have been much more extensive than it is ; but the spinners and manufacturers of Lancashire can as yet successfully compete with those of Lowell, though for how long a time remains to be seen, for the latter are yearly gaining experience and improving their machinery, so that before long they will be able to compete with the old country, more especially should the executive [*sic*] abolish the present protective system adopted with respect to the import of cotton manufactures." This was written in 1858.

coarse hairy one.   A process of careful sorting by hand must therefore be gone through before manufacture can begin.   In some branches of the industry the qualities of the fibre, and those of the goods which are to be made from it, call for more of manual labor, and admit in less degree of the use of machinery, than is the case with the cottons; and it is a familiar fact, though one of which the true meaning has not often been grasped, that a need of resorting to direct manual labor in large proportion and a difficulty in substituting machinery, constitute, under conditions of freedom, an obstacle to the profitable prosecution of a branch of industry in the United States.   But, on the other hand, certain qualities of wool are grown to advantage in the climate of this country and under its industrial conditions, especially strong merino wools of good though not fine grade, of comparatively short staple, adapted for the making of flannels, blankets, and substantial cloths.   At the same time, machinery can be applied to making these fabrics with less difficulty than to the manufacture of some finer goods.

Our information in regard to the history of the woollen manufacture is even more defective than that on iron and cottons.   For the period between 1830 and 1840 we have no information that is worth any thing.   In 1840 the industry was confined to making satinets (a substantial, inexpensive cloth, not of fine quality), broadcloths, flannels, and blankets.[1]   The tariff act of 1842 imposed on

---

[1] See a passage quoted from Wade's "Fibre and Fabric" in the Bureau of Statistics' "Report on Wool and Manufactures of Wool," 1887, p. xlvii.

woollen goods a duty of 40 per cent., and on wool one of three cents a pound plus 30 per cent. on the value. It is said that during the four years in which these rates were in force a stimulus was giving to the making of finer qualities of broadcloths, the development being aided by evasions of the *ad valorem* duty on wool.[1] The act, however, did not remain in force long enough to make it clear what would have been its permanent effect on the woollen manufacture. Whatever may have been the start made in these few years in making finer woollens, this branch of the industry, as is generally admitted, well-nigh disappeared under the duties of 1846. The tariff of that year imposed a duty of 30 per cent. on woollen goods in general; but flannels and worsteds were admitted at 25 per cent., and blankets at 20 per cent. On wool also the duty was 30 per cent. Under this arrangement of duties,—whether or not in consequence of it,—no development took place in those branches of the manufacture which needed wool that was subject to the 30 per cent. duty. The finest grades of woollens were not made at all. But the manufacture of cloths of ordinary quality (so-called cassimeres and similar goods), and that of blankets and flannels, continued to show a regular growth. The census figures are not of much value as accurate statistics, but there seems to be no reason for doubting that they prove a steady advance in the woollen manufac-

---

[1] Grosvenor. " Does Protection Protect ? " p. 147 ; Introduction to the volume of the " Census of 1860 " on Manufactures, p. xxxiii.

ture as a whole.[1] The growth was confined mostly to those branches which used domestic wool; but within these there was not only increase, but development. The methods of manufacture were improved, better machinery was introduced, and new kinds of goods were made.[2] It is a striking fact that the very high protective duties which were imposed during the civil war, and were increased after its close, have not brought the manufacture of woollen cloths to a position substantially different from that which had been attained before 1860. The description of the industry which the spokesman of the Asso-

---

[1] The census figures on the woollen manufacture are :

					Capital. (In million dollars.)	Value of Product.	Hands Employed.
1840	.	.	.	.	15.7	20.	21,342
1850	.	.	.	.	26.1	43.5	34,895
1860	.	.	.	.	30.8	61.9	41,360

The figures for 1850 are exclusive of those relating to blankets ; for 1860 are exclusive of those relating to worsteds.

[2] "Eighteen hundred and fifty saw the success of the Crompton loom at Lowell and Lawrence, on which were made a full line of Scotch plaids in all their beautiful colorings, as well as star twills, half-diamonds. * * * Up to that time fancy cassimeres had been made largely through the Blackstone Valley (in Rhode Island) on the Crompton and Tappet looms, as made by William Crompton. As early as 1846 the Jacquard was used at Woonsocket and Blackstone. From 1850 to 1860 fancy cassimeres made a rapid advance, and the styles ran to extremes far more than they have ever since." Wade's "Fibre and Fabric," as quoted above, p. xlviii.

According to the official "Statistical Information Relating to Certain Branches of Industry in Massachusetts," 1855, at pp. 573–575, woollen goods were made in 1855 in that State as follows :

Broadcloth to the value of	$ 838,000
Cassimeres to the value of	5,015,000
Satinets to the value of	2,709,000
Flannels and blankets to the value of . . .	3,126,000
Woollen yarns to the value of	386,000

ciation of Wool Manufacturers gave in 1884 is, in the main, applicable to its state in 1860. " The woollen manufacture of this country * * * is almost wholly absorbed in production for the masses. Nine tenths of our card-wool fabrics are made directly for the ready-made clothing establishments, by means of which most of the laboring people and all the boys are supplied with woollen garments. The manufacture of flannels, blankets, and ordinary knit goods—pure necessaries of life—occupies most of the other mills engaged in working up carded wool."[1]

Some outlying branches of the woollen manufacture, however, showed a striking advance during the period we are considering. The most noteworthy of these is the carpet manufacture, which received a great impetus from the application of newly-invented machinery. The power-loom for weaving ingrain carpets was invented in 1841 by Mr. E. B. Bigelow, and the more complicated loom for weaving Brussels carpets was first perfected by the same inventive genius in 1848.[2] The new machinery at

---

[1] Mr. John L. Hayes, in the " Bulletin of the Association of Wool Manufacturers," vol. xiv., p. 116. Mr. Hayes also states the woollen manufacture to be " capable of producing commodities of the highest luxury,—rich carpets, fine upholsteries, and superfine broadcloths " ; but his description of other branches of the industry is similar to that quoted in the text on card-wool goods. " The dress goods manufactured are fabricates almost exclusively for the million, the women of the exclusive and fashionable classes supplying themselves mainly through French importations. The vast carpet manufacture of Philadelphia, larger than in any city of Europe, has its chief occupation in furnishing carpets for the more modest houses."

[2] See the sketch of Mr. Bigelow's career up to 1854, in " Hunt's Merchants Magazine," xxx., pp. 162 170.

once put the manufacture of carpets on a firm basis ; and in its most important branches, the manufacture of ingrain and Brussels carpets, it became independent of aid from protective duties. A similar development took place in the manufacture of woollen hose. The knitting-frame had been invented in England as early as the sixteenth century, but had been worked only by hand. It was first adapted to machinery in the United States in 1831, and was first worked by machinery at Cohoes in New York in 1832. Other inventions followed ; and a prosperous industry developed, which supplied the entire domestic market, and was independent of protective duties.[1] On the other hand, hardly more than a beginning was made before the civil war in the manufacture of worsted goods. In 1860 there were no more than three considerable factories engaged in making worsteds, and the imports largely exceeded the domestic product.[2] Some ex-

---

[1] See the account of the history of the manufacture of knit goods in the "Census of 1860," volume on Manufactures, pp. xxxix.–xlv. Compare the brief sketch by John L. Hayes in his address on "Protection a Boon to Consumers" (Boston, 1867), pp. 9–11. No attempt had been made before 1860, in the United States or elsewhere, to make knit goods of cotton.

[2] See the Introduction to the volume on Manufactures, "Census of 1860," pp. xxxvi.–xxxix.

From the figures of production in the "Census of 1860," and from those of imports in the "Report on Commerce and Navigation" for the fiscal year 1859–60, we have the materials for a comparison of the domestic and the foreign supply of the most important kinds of woollen goods. The figures are :

	Production, 1860.	Imports, 1859-60.
Woollens generally (including flannels, but not blankets, shawls, or yarns) . : .	$43,500,000	$13,350,000
Carpets, ...	7,860,000	2,200,000
Worsteds	3,700,000	12,300,000

planation of this state of things may be found in the comparatively low duty of 25 per cent. on worsteds under the tariff of 1846. Something was due to the fact that the worsted industry in England not only was long established, but was steadily improving its methods and machinery. But the most important cause, doubtless, was the duty of 30 per cent. on the long-staple combing wool, which then was needed for making worsted goods, and which physical causes have prevented from being grown to any large extent in the United States.

The greatest difference between the woollen industry as it stands to-day and as it stood before 1860 is in the large worsted manufacture of the present, which has grown up almost entirely since the wool and woollens act of 1867. The high duties undoubtedly have been a cause of this development, or at least were so in the beginning; but a further and important cause has been the great improvement in combing machinery, which has rendered it possible to make so-called worsted goods from almost any grade of wool, and has largely done away with the distinction between woollen and worsted goods. The result has been that the worsted makers, as well as the makers of woollens, have been able to use domestic wool; and it is in the production of goods made of such wool that the greatest growth of recent years has taken place.

The tariff act of 1857 reduced the duty on woollens to 24 per cent., but much more than made up for this by admitting wool practically free of duty. Wool costing less than twenty cents at the place of exportation was admitted free, which amounted in effect to the exemption of almost all wool from duty. Moreover, dyestuffs and other materials were admitted free or at low rates. The free admission of wool from Canada, under the reciprocity treaty of 1854, had already been in force for three years.[1] The remission of duties on these materials explains the willingness with which the manufacturers in general acceded to the rearrangement of rates in 1857. In 1860, when the beginnings were made in re-imposing higher protective duties, it was admitted that no demand for such a change came from manufacturers.[2] The only exception was in the case of the iron-makers of Pennsylvania, who did not share in the benefits of the free list,

---

[1] Large quantities of combing wool were imported from Canada under the reciprocity treaty, and were used in making worsteds and carpets. In 1866, when the treaty was terminated, and high duties had been imposed on wool in general, the manufacturers pleaded hard for the continued free admission of Canada wool, though they were active in securing the general high duties of 1867 on wool and woollens. But they did not succeed in getting the Canada wools free. See the "Statement of Facts Relative to Canada Wools and the Manufacture of Worsteds," made by the National Association of Wool Manufacturers, Boston, 1866.

[2] Senator Hunter, who had been most active in bringing about the passage of the act of 1857, said, during the debate on the Morrill bill of 1860. "Have any of the manufacturers come here to complain or to ask for new duties? If they have, I am not aware of it, with the exception, perhaps, of a petition or two presented early in the session by the Senator from Connecticut. Is it not notorious that if we were to leave it to the manufacturers of New England themselves, to the manufacturers of hardware, textile fabrics, etc., there would be a large majority against any change? Do we not know that the woollen manufacture dates its revival from the tariff of 1857, which altered the duties on wool?" "Congressional Globe," 1859 –60, p. 301. Cp. the note to p. 160, below.

and who opposed the reduction of 1857. So far as the
manufacture of woollen goods was concerned, the
changes of 1857, as might have been expected, served
to stimulate the industry; and it grew and prospered
during the years immediately preceding the civil war.
A remission of duty on materials obviously operates
in the first instance mainly to the advantage of producers
and middle-men, and brings benefit to consumers only
by a more or less gradual process. The experiment of
free wool, with a moderate duty on woollens, was not tried ·
long enough to make certain what would be its final results. It is not impossible that, as is often asserted by
the opponents of duties on wool, the free admission of
that material would have led in time to a more varied
development of the woollen manufacture. On the other
hand, it may be, in the case of woollens as in that of cottons, that the conditions in the United States are less
favorable for making the finer qualities than for making
those cheaper qualities to which the application of machinery is possible in greater degree, and for which, at the
same time, the domestic wool is an excellent material.
The test of experience under conditions of freedom could
alone decide what are the real causes of the comparatively
limited range of both of the great textile industries; but
it is not improbable that general causes like those just
mentioned, rather than the hampering of the supply of
wool, account for the condition of the woollen manufacture. However that may be, it seems certain that the

practical remission of duty in 1857, whether or no it would in the long run have caused a wide development of the woollen manufacture, gave it for the time being a distinct stimulus; it seems to have had but little, if any, effect on the prices of domestic wool [1]; and it must have tended at the least to cheapen for the consumer goods made in whole or in part of foreign wool.

It would be possible to extend this inquiry farther, [2] but enough has been said for the present purpose. In the main, the changes in duties have had much less effect on the protected industries than is generally supposed. Their growth has been steady and continuous, and seems to have been little stimulated by the high duties of 1842, and little checked by the more moderate duties of 1846 and 1857. Probably the duties of the last-mentioned years, while on their face protective duties, did not have in any important degree the effect of stimulating indus-

---

[1] The price per pound of medium wool, averaged from quarterly quotations, was :

	cts.			cts.
In 1852 . .	38½	In 1856 . .		45
" 1853 . .	53	" 1857 . .		46
" 1854 . .	42½	" 1858 . .		36
" 1855 . .	38	" 1859 . .		47
		" 1860 . .		47½

The prices of other grades moved similarly. The panic of 1857 caused a fall in 1858, but in the following year the old level was recovered. The figures are based on the tables of wool prices in the Bureau of Statistics' " Report on Wool and Manufactures of Wool," 1887, p. 109. The movement of wool prices abroad during these years seems to have been about the same.

[2] In the Introduction to the volume on Manufactures of the "Census of 1860," to which reference has been made before, there is a useful sketch of the history of various branches of manufacture up to that date.

tries that could not have maintained themselves under freedom of trade. They did not operate as strictly protective duties, and did not bring that extra tax on consumers which is the peculiar effect of protective duties. The only industry which presents a marked exception to these general conditions is the manufacture of the cruder forms of iron. In that industry, the conditions of production in the eastern part of the United States were such that the protective duties of 1842 caused a return to old processes, and an enhanced price to the country without a corresponding gain to producers. Even under the rates of 1846 and after the use of anthracite coal, the same effect can be seen, though in less degree.

We often hear it said that any considerable reduction from the scale of duties in the present tariff, whose character and history will be considered in the following pages, would bring about the disappearance of manufacturing industries, or at least a disastrous check to their development. But the experience of the period before 1860 shows that predictions of this sort have little warrant. At present, as before 1860, the great textile manufactures are not dependent to any great extent on protective duties of the kind now imposed. The direction of their growth has been somewhat affected by these duties, yet in a less degree than might have been expected. It is striking that both under the system of high protection which has been maintained since the civil war, and under the more moderate system that preceded it, the cotton

and woollen industries have been kept in the main to
those goods of common use and large consumption to
which the economic conditions of the United States
might be expected to lead them. The same would
doubtless be found to be true of other branches of manufacture. In some cases, no doubt, their growth has
been stimulated beyond the point at which they
could maintain themselves under conditions of freedom. The making of pig-iron in the eastern part of the
United States now presents in some degree the case of
an industry dependent on a protective duty. Yet the
bulk even of the manufacture of crude iron would not be
likely to disappear under duties much lower than the present, or even in entire absence of duties. In general, the
extent to which mechanical branches of production have
been brought into existence and maintained by the protective system is greatly exaggerated by its advocates;
and even the character and direction of their development
have been influenced less than, on grounds of general
reasoning, might have been expected.

THE HISTORY OF THE EXISTING TARIFF.

CHAPTER I.

THE WAR TARIFF.

EVERY one has heard of our "war tariff" and of our "war taxes." Every one knows that our tariff is connected in some way with the series of extraordinary financial measures which the Rebellion called out. But few have any exact knowledge of the extent to which our extreme protective system is due to the war. An account of the way in which the tariff was put into its present shape will show how the exigencies of the Civil War caused duties to be greatly increased; how these high duties were retained and even increased in an unexpected and indefensible way; and how the tariff, as it now stands, is still, in the main, a product of war legislation. A history of the existing tariff is simply a history of the way in which the war duties were retained, increased, and systematized, and of the half-hearted and unsuccessful attempts at reduction and reform which have been made from time to time.

Before the war we had a tariff of duties which, though
The tariff not arranged completely or consistently on the
before the principles of free trade, was yet very moderate
war. in comparison with the existing system.   For
about fifteen years before the Rebellion began, duties
on imports were fixed by the acts of 1846 and 1857.
The act of 1846 had been passed by the Democratic
party with the avowed intention of putting into operation, as far as was possible, the principles of free
trade.   This intention, it is true, was by no means carried out consistently.   Purely revenue articles, like tea
and coffee, were admitted free of duty; and on the other
hand, articles like iron and manufactures of iron, cotton
goods, wool, and woollen goods,—in fact most of the important articles with which the protective controversy has
been concerned,—were charged with a duty of thirty per
cent.   Other articles again, like steel, copper, lead, were
admitted at a lower duty than this, not for any reasons of
revenue, but because they were not then produced to any
extent within the country, and because protection for
them in consequence was not asked.   Protection was by
no means absent from the act of 1846; and the rate of
thirty per cent., which it imposed on the leading articles,
would be supposed, in almost any civilized country, to
give even a high degree of protection.   Nevertheless, the
tariff of 1846 was, in comparison with the present tariff, a
moderate measure; and a return to its rates would now
be considered a great step of reform by those who are op-

posed to protective duties. The act of 1857 took away still more from the restrictive character of our tariff legislation. Congress, it may be remarked, acted in 1857 with reasonable soberness and impartiality, and without being influenced by political considerations. The maximum protective duty was reduced to twenty-four per cent.; many raw materials were admitted free; and the level of duties on the whole line of manufactured articles was brought down to the lowest point which has been reached in this country since 1815. It is not likely we shall see, for a great many years to come, a nearer approach to the free-trade ideal.

The country accepted the tariff acts of 1846 and 1857, and was satisfied with them. Except in the years immediately following the passage of the former act, when there was some attempt to induce a return to a more rigid protective system, agitation on the tariff ceased almost entirely. There is no doubt that the period from 1846 to 1860 was a time of great material prosperity, interrupted, but not checked, by the crisis of 1857. It would be going too far to assert that this general prosperity was due chiefly to the liberal character of the tariff. Other causes exercised a great and perhaps a predominant influence. But the moderate tariff undoubtedly was one of the elements that contributed to the general welfare. It may be well to add that prosperity was not confined to any part of the country, or to any branches of industry. Manufactures in general continued to flourish; and the

reduction of duties which was made in 1857 had the consent and approbation of the main body of the manufacturing class.

The crisis of 1857 had caused a falling off in the revenue from duties. This was made the occasion for a reaction from the liberal policy of 1846 and 1857. In 1861
the Morrill tariff act began a change toward a higher range
of duties and a stronger application of protection. The
Morrill act is often spoken of as if it were the basis of the
present protective system. But this is by no means the
The Morrill case. The tariff act of 1861 was passed by the
tariff act House of Representatives in the session of
of 1861. 1859–60, the session preceding the election of
President Lincoln. It was passed, undoubtedly, with
the intention of attracting to the Republican party,
at the approaching Presidential election, votes in Pennsylvania and other States that had protectionist leanings. In the Senate the tariff bill was not taken
up in the same session in which it was passed in the
House. Its consideration was postponed, and it was not
until the next session—that of 1860–61—that it received
the assent of the Senate and became law. It is clear that
the Morrill tariff was carried in the House before any
serious expectation of war was entertained; and it was
accepted by the Senate in the session of 1861 without
material change. It therefore forms no part of the financial legislation of the war, which gave rise in time to a
series of measures that entirely superseded the Morrill

tariff. Indeed, Mr. Morrill and the other supporters of
the act of 1861 declared that their intention was simply
to restore the rates of 1846. The important change
which they proposed to make from the provisions of the
tariff of 1846 was to substitute specific for *ad-valorem*
duties. Such a change from *ad-valorem* to specific
duties is in itself by no means objectionable; but it has
usually been made a pretext on the part of protectionists
for a considerable increase in the actual duties paid.
When protectionists make a change of this kind, they
almost invariably make the specific duties higher than the
ad-valorem duties for which they are supposed to be an
equivalent,—a circumstance which has given rise to the
common notion, of course unfounded, that there is some
essential connection between free trade and *ad-valorem*
duties on the one hand, and between protection and
specific duties on the other hand. The Morrill tariff
formed no exception to the usual course of things in this
respect. The specific duties which it established were in
many cases considerably above the *ad-valorem* duties of
1846. The most important direct changes made by the
act of 1861 were in the increased duties on iron and on
wool, by which it was hoped to attach to the Republican
party Pennsylvania and some of the Western States.
Most of the manufacturing States at this time still stood
aloof from the movement toward higher rates.[1]

---

[1] Mr. Rice, of Massachusetts, said in 1860 : " The manufacturer asks no
additional protection. He has learned, among other things, that the great-

Hardly had the Morrill tariff act been passed when Fort Sumter was fired on. The Civil War began. The need of additional revenue for carrying on the great struggle was immediately felt; and as early as the extra session of the summer of 1861, additional customs duties were imposed. In the next regular session, in December, 1861, a still further increase of duties was made. From that time till 1865 no session, indeed, hardly a month of any session, passed in which some increase of duties on imports was not made. During the four years of the war every resource was strained for carrying on the great struggle. Probably no country has seen, in so short a time, so extraordinary a mass of financial legislation. A huge national debt was accumulated; the mischievous expedient of an inconvertible paper currency was resorted to; a national banking system unexpectedly arose from the confusion; an enormous system of internal taxation was created; the duties on imports were vastly increased and extended. We are concerned here only with the change in the tariff; yet it must be borne in mind that

---

est evil, next to a ruinous competition from foreign sources, is an excessive protection, which stimulates a like ruinous and irresponsible competition at home,"—*Congress. Globe*, 1859–60, p. 1867. Mr. Sherman said: "When Mr. Stanton says the manufacturers are urging and pressing this bill, he says what he must certainly know is not correct. The manufacturers have asked over and over again to be let alone. The tariff of 1857 is the manufacturers' bill; but the present bill is more beneficial to the agricultural interest than the tariff of 1857."—*Ibid.*, p. 2053. *Cf.* Hunter's Speech, *Ibid.*, p. 3010. In later years Mr. Morrill himself said that the tariff of 1861 "was not asked for, and but coldly welcomed, by manufacturers, who always and justly fear instability."—*Congr. Globe*, 1869–70, p. 3295.

these changes were only a part of the great financial measures which the war called out.   Indeed, it is impossible to
understand the meaning of the changes which were made
in the tariff without a knowledge of the other legislation
that accompanied it, and more especially of the extended
system of internal taxation which was adopted at the
same time.   To go through the various acts for levying
internal taxes and imposing duties on imports is not necessary in order to make clear the character and bearing of
the legislation of the war.   It will be enough to describe
those that are typical and important.   The great acts of
1862 and 1864 are typical of the whole course of the war
measures; and the latter is of particular importance,
because it became the foundation of the existing tariff
system.

It was not until 1862 that the country began to appreciate how great must be the efforts necessary to suppress
the Rebellion, and that Congress set to work in earnest to
provide the means for that purpose.   Even in 1862 Congress relied more on selling bonds and on issuing paper-
money than on immediate taxation.   But Tax and
two vigorous measures were resorted to for tariff acts of
taxing the people immediately and directly. 1862.
The first of these was the internal revenue act of
July 1, 1862.   This established a comprehensive system
of excise taxation.   Specific taxes were imposed on
the production of iron and steel, coal-oil, paper, leather,
and other articles.   A general *ad-valorem* tax was

imposed on other manufactures. In addition, licenses were required in many callings. A general income tax was imposed. Railroad companies, steamboats, express companies were made to pay taxes on their gross receipts. Those who have grown to manhood within the last fifteen years find it difficult to imagine the existence and to appreciate the burden of this heavy and vexatious mass of taxation; for it was entirely swept away within a few years after the end of the war.

The second great measure of taxation to which Congress turned at this time was the tariff act of July 14, 1862. The object of this act, as was stated by Messrs. Morrill and Stevens, who had charge of its passage in the House, was primarily to increase duties only to such an extent as might be necessary in order to offset the internal taxes of the act of July 1st.[1] But although this was the chief object of the act, protective intentions were entertained by those who framed it, and were carried out. Both Messrs. Morrill and Stevens were avowed protectionists, and did not conceal that they meant in many cases to help the home producer. The increase of duties on articles which were made in this country was therefore,

---

[1] Mr. Morrill said, in his speech introducing the tariff bill: "It will be indispensable for us to revise the tariff on foreign imports, so far as it may be seriously disturbed by any internal duties, and to make proper reparation. * * * If we bleed manufacturers, we must see to it that the proper tonic is administered at the same time."—*Congr. Globe*, 1861-62, p. 1196. Similarly Mr. Stevens said: "We intended to impose an additional duty on imports equal to the tax which had been put on the domestic articles. It was done by way of compensation to domestic manufacturers against foreign importers."—*Ibid.*, p. 2979.

in all cases, at least sufficient to afford the domestic producers compensation for the internal taxes which they had
to pay. In many cases it was more than sufficient for this
purpose, and brought about a distinct increase of protection. Had not the internal revenue act been passed,
affording a good reason for some increase of duties; had
not the higher taxation of purely revenue articles, like
tea and coffee, been a justifiable and necessary expedient
for increasing the government income; had not the
increase even of protective duties been quite defensible as
a temporary means for the same end ; had not the general
feeling been in favor of vigorous measures for raising the
revenue;—had these conditions not existed, it would have
been very difficult to carry through Congress a measure
like the tariff of 1862. But, as matters stood, the tariff
was easily passed. Under cover of the need of revenue
and of the intention to prevent domestic producers from
being unfairly handicapped by the internal taxes, a clear
increase of protection was in many cases brought about.

The war went on; still more revenue was needed.
Gradually Congress became convinced of the necessity of
resorting to still heavier taxation, and of the willingness
of the country to pay all that was necessary to maintain
the Union. Passing over less important acts, we have to
consider the great measure that was the climax of the
financial legislation of the war. The three revenue acts
of June 30, 1864, practically form one measure, and that
probably the greatest measure of taxation which the

world has seen. The first of the acts provided for an enormous extension of the internal-tax system; the second for a corresponding increase of the duties on imports; the third authorized a loan of $400,000,000.

The internal revenue act was arranged, as Mr. David

Internal revenue act, 1864.

A. Wells has said, on the principle of the Irishman at Donnybrook fair; "Whenever you see a head, hit it; whenever you see a commodity, tax it." Every thing was taxed, and taxed heavily. Every ton of pig-iron produced was charged two dollars; every ton of railroad iron three dollars; sugar paid two cents a pound; salt, six cents a hundred-weight. The general tax on all manufactures produced was five per cent. But this tax was repeated on almost every article in different stages of production. Raw cotton, for instance, was taxed two cents a pound; as cloth, it again paid five per cent. Mr. Wells estimates that the government in fact collected between eight and fifteen per cent. on every finished product. Taxes on the gross receipts of railroad, steamboat, telegraph, express, and insurance companies were levied, or were increased where already in existence. The license-tax system was extended to almost every conceivable branch of trade. The income tax was raised to five per cent. on moderate incomes, and to ten per cent. on incomes of more than $10,000.

Tariff act of 1864.

The tariff act of 1864, passed at the same time with the internal revenue act, also brought about a great increase in the rates of taxation. Like the tariff act

of 1862, that of 1864 was introduced, explained, amended,
and passed under the management of Mr. Morrill, who
was Chairman of the Committee on Ways and Means. That
gentleman again stated, as he had done in 1862, that the
passage of the tariff act was rendered necessary in order
to put domestic producers in the same situation, so far as
foreign competition was concerned, as if the internal taxes
had not been raised. This was one great object of the
new tariff ; and it may have been a good reason for bringing forward some measure of the kind. But it explains
only in part the measure which in fact was proposed and
passed. The tariff of 1864 was a characteristic result of
that veritable furor of taxation which had become fixed
in the minds of the men who were then managing the
national finances. Mr. Morrill, and those who with him
made our revenue laws, seem to have had but one principle : to tax every possible article indiscriminately, and to
tax it at the highest rates that any one had the courage to
suggest. They carried this method out to its fullest
extent in the tariff act of 1864, as well as in the tax act of
that year. At the same time these statesmen were protectionists, and did not attempt to conceal their protectionist leanings. What between their willingness to make
every tax and duty as high as possible for the sake of
raising revenue, and their belief that high import duties
were beneficial to the country, the protectionists had an
opportunity such as the country has never before given
them. It would be unfair to say that Mr. Morrill, Mr.

Stevens, and the other gentlemen who shaped the revenue laws, consciously used the urgent need of money for the war as a means of carrying out their protectionist theories, or of promoting, through high duties, private ends for themselves or others. But it is certain that their method of treating the revenue problems resulted in a most unexpected and extravagant application of protection, and moreover, made possible a subservience of the public needs to the private gains of individuals such as unfortunately made its appearance in many other branches of the war administration. Every domestic producer who came before Congress got what he wanted in the way of duties. Protection ran riot; and this, moreover, not merely for the time being. The whole tone of the public mind toward the question of import duties became distorted. Not only during the war, but for several years after it, all feeling of opposition to high import duties almost entirely disappeared. The habit of putting on as high rates as any one asked had become so strong that it could hardly be shaken off; and even after the war, almost any increase of duties demanded by domestic producers was readily made. The war had in many ways a bracing and ennobling influence on our national life; but its immediate effect on business affairs, and on all legislation affecting moneyed interests, was demoralizing. The line between public duty and private interests was often lost sight of by legislators. Great fortunes were made by changes in legislation urged and brought about by those who were

benefited by them; and the country has seen with sorrow
that the honor and honesty of public men did not remain
undefiled. The tariff, like other legislation on matters of
finance, was affected by these causes. Schemes for money-
making were incorporated in it, and were hardly ques-
tioned by Congress. When more enlightened and
unselfish views began to make their way, and protests
were made against the abuses and excessive duties of the
war period, these had obtained, as we shall see, too strong
a hold to be easily shaken off.

Such were the conditions under which the tariff act of
1864 was passed. As in 1862, three causes were at work:
in the first place, the urgent need of revenue for the war;
in the next, the wish to offset the internal taxes imposed
on domestic producers; and finally, the protectionist
leanings of those who managed our financial legislation.
These causes made possible a tariff act which in ordinary
times would have been summarily rejected. It raised
duties greatly and indiscriminately,—so much so, that the
average rate on dutiable commodities, which had been
37.2 per cent. under the act of 1862, became 47.06 per
cent. under that of 1864. It was in many ways crude
and ill-considered; it established protective duties more
extreme than had been ventured on in any previous tariff
act in our country's history; it contained flagrant abuses,
in the shape of duties whose chief effect was to bring
money into the pockets of private individuals.

Nothing more clearly illustrates the character of this

piece of legislation, and the circumstances which made its enactment a possibility, than the public history of its passage through Congress.   The bill was introduced into the House on June 2d by Mr. Morrill.   General debate on it was stopped after one day.   The House then proceeded to the consideration of amendments.   Almost without exception amendments offered by Mr. Morrill were adopted, and all others were rejected.   After two days had been given in this way to the amendments, the House, on June 4th, passed the bill.   In the Senate much the same course was followed.   The consideration of the bill began on June 16th ; it was passed on the following day.   That is to say, five days in all were given by the two houses to this act, which was in its effects one of the most important financial measures ever passed in the United States.   The bill was accepted as it came from the Committee on Ways and Means, and was passed practically without debate or examination.   No pretence could be made of any detailed or effective criticism by Congress.

The necessity of the situation, the critical state of the country, the urgent need of revenue, may have justified this haste, which, it is safe to say, is unexampled in the The tariff   history of civilized countries.   But surely there of 1864 is the   can be no excuse for making a measure passed basis of   in this manner and under these circumstances the existing   tariff.   the foundation of the permanent economic policy of an enlightened people.   And yet this has been the case, and it is the central point in the history of tariff legislation of the last twenty-five years. The tariff act of 1864 is the basis of the existing system of import duties. Great changes have indeed been made since the war, as will be seen in the following chapters. But on almost all the articles with which the protective controversy is concerned, rates are still those of the tariff act of 1864. This is said without taking into account the last tariff act, that of 1883; and it will be seen at a subsequent point that the changes made by the act of 1883 were not of sufficient importance to affect the substantial correctness of the general statement. In regard to the duties as they stood before 1883, it is literally true, in regard to almost all protected articles, that the tariff act of 1864 remained in force for twenty years without reductions. Any one who will glance over the margin of those sections of the Revised Statutes of the United States which refer to the tariff, can see how large a proportion of the rates there enumerated date from the year 1864; and if he notes the occasional protective duties set down in the Revised Statutes as having been fixed by acts passed later than 1864, he will find that these almost invariably show, not a reduction, but an increase over the rates of the war tariff. [1]

---

[1] In Heyl's " Import Duties " the reader will find the act of 1864 printed in full, those parts which are no longer in force being distinguished by small type, and he will be surprised to find (in any edition before 1883, how few sections of the act are set down as obsolete. See, *e g.*, edition of 1879, pp. 57-73.

It should be said that the act of 1864 was not in form a general act, repealing all previous enactments. It left in force, for instance, all pro-

How this maintenance of the war duties came about, will be the subject of the following chapters.

---

visions of the Morrill act of 1861 and of the tariff act of 1862 which were not expressly changed by it.   But it affected so completely and with so few exceptions the whole range of import duties, and especially the protective duties, that it was practically a new general tariff.

CHAPTER II.

THE FAILURE TO REDUCE THE TARIFF AFTER THE WAR.

WHEN the war closed, the revenue acts which had been hastily passed during its course constituted a chaotic mass. Congress and the Secretary of the Treasury immediately set to work to bring some order into this chaos, by funding and consolidating the debt, by contracting the paper currency, and by reforming and reducing the internal taxes.[1] The years between 1865 and 1870 are full of discussions and enactments on taxation and finance. On some parts of the financial system, in regard to which there was little disagreement, action was prompt and salutary. The complicated mass of internal taxes was felt to be an evil by all. It bore heavily and vexatiously on the people ; and Congress proceeded to sweep it away with all possible speed. As soon as the immense floating debt had been funded, and the extent of the

---

[1] Those who wish to get some knowledge of the confused character of the financial legislation called out by the war, are referred to Mr. David A. Wells's excellent essay on "The Recent Financial Experiences of the United States " (1872). Those who wish to study more in detail the course of events after the war should read Mr. Wells's reports as Commissioner of the Revenue, of 1867, 1868, 1869, and 1870.

annual needs of the government became somewhat clear,
Congress set to work at repealing and modifying the excise
laws.   It is not necessary to enumerate the various steps
Abolition   by which the internal-tax system was modi-
of the   fied.   Year after year acts for reducing and
internal taxes abolishing internal taxes were passed.   By 1872
1866–1872.
               all those which had any connection with the
subject of our investigation—the protective duties—
had disappeared.[1]   The taxes on spirits and beer,
those on banks, and a few comparatively unimportant
taxes on matches, patent medicines, and other articles
were retained.   But all those taxes which bore heavily on
the productive resources of the country—those taxes
in compensation for which higher duties had been imposed in 1862 and 1864—were entirely abolished.

Step by step with this removal of the internal taxes, a
reduction of import duties should have taken place ; at
the least, a reduction which would have taken off those
additional duties that had been put on in order to offset
the internal taxes.   This, however, Congress hesitated to
undertake.   We have seen in the preceding chapter that
the opportunity given by the war system of taxation was
seized by the protectionists in order to carry out their
wishes.   It would not be easy to say whether at the time
the public men who carried out this legislation meant the
new system of import duties to be permanent.   Certainly
the war methods of finance as a whole were not meant to

---

[1] The most important acts for reducing the internal taxes were those of July
11, 1866 ; March 2, 1867 ; March 31, 1868 ; July 14, 1870 ; June 6, 1872.

remain in force for an unlimited time. Some parts of the tariff were beyond doubt intended to be merely temporary; and the reasonable expectation was that the protective duties would sooner or later be overhauled and reduced. Had the question been directly put to almost any public man, whether the tariff system of the war was to be continued, the answer would certainly have been in the negative,—that in due time the import duties were to be lowered.[1] During the years of confusion immediately after the war little was attempted; but soon a disposition to affect some reform in the incongruous mass of duties began to be shown. Each year schemes for reduction and reform were brought forward. Commissions were appointed, bills were elaborated and considered; but the reform was put off from year to year. The pressure from the interested domestic producers was strong; the power of the lobby was great; the overshadowing problem of reconstruction absorbed the energies of Congress. Gradu-

[1] As late as 1870, Mr. Morrill said : " For revenue purposes, and not solely for protection, fifty per cent. in many instances has been added to the tariff [during the war] to enable our home trade to bear the new but indispensable burdens of internal taxation. Already we have relinquished most of such taxes. So far, then, as protection is concerned * * * we might safely remit a percentage of the tariff on a considerable share of our foreign importations. * * * *It is a mistake of the friends of a sound tariff to insist on the extreme rates impo ed during the war*, if less will raise the necessary revenue. * * * Whatever percentage of duties was imposed on foreign goods to cover internal taxation on home manufactures, should not now be claimed as the lawful prize of protection, when such taxes have been repealed. There is no longer an equivalent."—*Congress. Globe*, 1869–70, p. 3295. These passages occur at the end of a long speech in favor of the principle of protection.

ally, as the organization of industry in the country adapted itself more closely to the tariff as it was, the feeling that no reform was needed obtained a strong hold. Many industries had grown up, or had been greatly extended, under the influence of the war legislation. As that legislation continued unchanged, still more capital was embarked in establishments whose existence or prosperity was in some degree dependent on its maintenance. All who were connected with establishments of this kind asserted that they would be ruined by any change. The business world in general tends to be favorable to the maintenance of things as they are. The country at large, and especially those parts of it in which the protected industries were concentrated, began to look on the existing state of things as permanent. The extreme protective system, which had been at the first a temporary expedient for aiding in the struggle for the Union, adopted hastily and without any thought of deliberation, gradually became accepted as a permanent institution. From this it was a short step, in order to explain and justify the existing state of things, to set up high protection as a theory and a dogma. The restraint of trade with foreign countries, by means of import duties of forty, fifty, sixty, even a hundred per cent., came to be advocated as a good thing in itself by many who, under normal circumstances, would have thought such a policy preposterous. Ideas of this kind were no longer the exploded errors of a small school of economists; they became the foundation of the policy of a great people. Then the mass of restrictive legislation which had been hurriedly piled up during the war, was strengthened and completed, and made into a firm and consistent edifice. On purely revenue articles, such as are not produced at all in the country, the duties were almost entirely abolished. A few raw materials, it is true, were admitted at low rates, or entirely free of duty. But these were exceptions, made apparently by accident. As a rule, the duties on articles produced in the country, that is, the protective duties, were retained at the war figures, or raised above them. The result was that the tariff gradually became exclusively and distinctly a protective measure; it included almost all the protective duties put on during the war, added many more to them, and no longer contained the purely revenue duties of the war.

We turn now to a somewhat more detailed account of the process by which the reform of the tariff was prevented. To give a complete account of the various tariff acts which were passed, or of the tariff bills which were pressed without success, is needless. Every session of Congress had its array of tariff acts and tariff bills; and we may content ourselves with an account of those which are typical of the general course of events. Of the attempts at reform which were made in the years immediately after the war, the fate of the tariff Unsuccessful bills of 1867 is characteristic. Two proposals tariff bill were then before Congress: one a bill passed of 1867. by the House at the previous session; the other a bill

prepared by Mr. David A. Wells, then Special Commissioner of the Revenue, and heartily approved by
Secretary McCulloch. The great rise in prices and in
money wages in these years, and the industrial embarrassment which followed the war, had caused a demand
for still higher import duties; the House bill had been
framed to answer this demand, and proposed a general
increase. Mr. Wells recommended a different policy.
He had not then become convinced of the truth of the
principles of free trade ; but he had clearly seen that the
indiscriminate protection which the war tariff gave, and
which the House bill proposed to augment, could not be
beneficial. His bill reduced duties on raw materials, such
as scrap-iron, coal, lumber, hemp, and flax ; and it either
maintained without change or slightly lowered the duties
on most manufactured articles. A careful rearrangement
was at the same time made in the rates on spices, chemi-
cals, dyes, and dye-woods,—articles of which a careful
and detailed examination is necessary for the determina-
tion of duties, and in regard to which the tariff contained
then, as it does now, much that was arbitrary and indefensible. Mr. Wells's bill, making these reforms, gained
the day over the less liberal House bill. It was passed by
the Senate, as an amendment to the House bill, by a large
majority (27 to 10). In the House there was also a majority in its favor ; but unfortunately a two-thirds majority was necessary in order to suspend the rules and bring
it before the House. The vote was 106 to 64 in favor of

the bill; the two-thirds majority was not obtained, and it failed to become law. The result was not only that no general tariff bill was passed at this session, but the course of tariff reform for the future received a regrettable check. Had Mr. Wells's proposals been enacted, it is not unlikely that the events of the next few years would have been very different from what in fact they were. It would be too much to say that these proposals looked forward to still further steps in the way of moderating the protective system, or that their favorable reception showed any distinct tendency against protection. There was at that time no free-trade feeling at all, and Mr. Wells's bill was simply a reform measure from the protectionist point of view. But the vote on it is nevertheless significant of the fact that the extreme and uncompromising protective spirit was not then all-powerful. The bill, it is true, had been modified in a protectionist direction in various ways before it came to be voted on; but the essential reductions and reforms were still contained in it and the votes show that the protectionist feeling was far from being solidified at that time to the extent that it came to be a few years later. Had the bill of 1867 been passed, the character of recent tariff legislation might have been very different. A beginning would have been made in looking at the tariff from a sober point of view, and in reducing duties that were clearly pernicious. The growing habit of looking on the war rates as a permanent system might have been checked, and the attempts at tariff reform in subse-

quent years would probably have found stronger support
and met with less successful opposition.   From this time
till the tariff act of 1883 was passed, there was no general
tariff bill which had so good a chance of being passed.
The failure of the attempt of 1867 encouraged the protectionists in fighting for the retention of the war duties
wherever they could not secure an increase over and
above them ; and in this contest they were, with few
exceptions, successful.[1]

Of the legislation that was in fact carried out, the act of
Act of 1870. 1870 is a fair example. It was passed in compliance with the demand for a reduction of taxes and for tariff reform, which was at that time especially strong in the
West, and was there made alike by Republicans and Democrats.[2] The declared intention of those who framed it and

[1] Mr. Wells's bill and the rates proposed in the House bill may be found
in his report for 1866-67, pp. 235-290. The principle of "enlightened
protection" on which he proceeded is stated on p. 34. At this time Mr.
Wells was still a protectionist ; it was not until he prepared his report for
1868-69 that he showed himself fully convinced of the unsoundness of the
theory of protection.   His able investigations and the matter-of-fact tone of
all of his reports gave much weight to his change of opinion, and caused it
to strengthen greatly the public feeling in favor of tariff reform.

[2] President Garfield (then Representative) said in 1870 : " After studying
the whole subject as carefully as I am able, I am firmly of the opinion that
the wisest thing that the protectionists in this House can do is to unite on a
moderate reduction of duties on imported articles.   *   *   *   If I do not
misunderstand the signs of the times, unless we do this ourselves, prudently
and wisely, we shall before long be compelled to submit to a violent reduction, made rudely and without discrimination, which will shock, if not
shatter, all our protected industries."—Young's Report, p. clxxii. It is
worthy of remark that Mr. Garfield had also supported earnestly the unsuccessful bill of 1867. He had appealed to his party to vote so as to make up
the two-thirds majority necessary for its consideration, telling them that later

had charge of it in Congress was to reduce taxation. But the reductions made by it were, almost without exception, on purely revenue articles. The duties on tea, coffee, wines, sugar, molasses, and spices were lowered. Other articles of the same kind were put on the free list. The only noteworthy reduction in the protective parts of the tariff was in the duty on pig-iron, which went down from $9.00 to $7.00 a ton. On the other hand, a very considerable increase of duties was made on a number of protected articles—on steel rails, on marble, on nickel, and on other articles.[1] We shall have occasion to refer to some of these indefensible exactions in another connection.[2] At present we are concerned only with the reductions of duty which were carried out. Among the protective duties the lowering of that on pig-iron was the only one of importance. This change, indeed, might well have been made at an earlier date, for the internal tax of $2.00 on pig-iron (in compensation for which the tariff rate had been raised to $9.00 in 1864) had been taken off as early as 1866.[3]

The only effort to reform the protective parts of the tariff which had any degree of success, was made in

---

they might "make up their record" by voting against it.—*Congr. Globe,* 1866-67, pp. 1657, 1658.

[1] An increase in the duties on bar-iron was also proposed in the bill as reported by the Committee on Ways and Means; but this, fortunately, was more than could be carried through. See the speeches of Messrs. Brooks (*Congr. Globe,* 1869-70, part 7, appendix, pp. 163-167) and Allison (*ibid.,* p. 192 *et seq.*). which protest against the sham reductions of the bill.

[2] See chapter iii.

[3] See the list of reductions made by the act of 1870 in Young's Report, p. clxxvii.

1872. The tactics of the proctectionists in that year illustrate strikingly the manner in which attempts at tariff reform have been frustrated ; and the history of the attempt is, from this point of view, so instructive that it may be told somewhat in detail. The situation
Situation in 1872 was in many ways favorable for tariff
1872. reform. The idea of tax and tariff reform was familiar to the people at large. It was not as yet openly pretended that the protective duties were to remain indefinitely as they had been fixed in the war. The act of 1870 had made a concession by the reduction on pig-iron; further changes of the same kind were expected to follow. Moreover, the feeling in favor of tariff reform was in all these years particularly strong in the West. So strong was it that, as has already been noted, it overrode party differences, and made almost all the Western Congressmen, whether Democrats or Republicans, act in favor of reductions in the tariff. The cause of this state of things is to be found in the economic condition of the country from the end of the war till after the panic of 1873. The prices of manufactured goods were then high, and imports were large. On the other hand, exports were comparatively small and the prices of grain and provisions low. The agricultural population was far from prosperous. The granger movement, and the agitation against the railroads, were one result of the depressed condition of the farmers. Another result was the strong feeling against the tariff, which the farmers

rightly believed to be among the causes of the state of things under which they were suffering.[1] Their representatives in Congress were therefore compelled to take a stand in favor of lowering the protective duties. The Western members being nearly all agreed on this subject, Congress contained a clear majority in favor of a reform in the tariff. Party lines at that time had little influence on the protective controversy, and, although both houses were strongly Republican, a strong disposition showed itself in both in favor of measures for lowering the protective duties.

Added to all this, the state of the finances demanded immediate attention. The redundant revenue, which has forced Congress in the last two or three years to pay attention to the question of tariff reform, had the same influence in 1872. In each of the fiscal years, 1870–71 and 1871–72, the surplus revenue, after paying all appropriations and all interest on the public debt, amounted to about $100,000,000, a sum greatly in excess of any requirements of the sinking fund. The government was buying bonds in the open market in order to dispose of the money that was flowing into the treasury vaults.[2]

---

[1] No satisfactory investigation of the period preceding the crisis of 1873 has yet been made. Of the fact that the situation was especially depressing for the agricultural parts of the country, there can be no doubt. The speculative mania and the fictitious prosperity of those years were felt most strikingly in manufactures and railroad building ; exactly why so little effect of this appeared in agriculture has never been clearly explained. The whole period will repay careful economic study.

[2] On account of the low premium on bonds and the high premium on gold,

This being the state of affairs, the Committee on Ways and Means introduced into the House a bill which took decided steps in the direction of tariff reform. Mr. Dawes, of Massachusetts, the chairman of the committee, was opposed to the recommendations of the majority of its members, and therefore left the explanation and management of the bill to Mr. Finkelnburg, of Missouri. That gentleman explained that the committee's measure was intended merely to " divest some industries of the superabundant protection which smells of monoply, and which it was never intended they should enjoy after the war." [1] The bill lopped off something from the protective duties in almost all directions. Pig-iron was to be charged $6.00 instead of $7.00 a ton. The duties on wool and woollens, and those on cottons, were to be reduced by about twenty per cent. Coal, salt, and lumber were subjected to lower duties. Tea and coffee were also to pay less; but the duties on them were not entirely abolished,—a circumstance which it is important to note in connection with subsequent events. The bill still left an ample measure of protection subsisting; but it was clearly intended to bring about an appreciable and permanent reduction of the war duties.

This bill was introduced into the House in April. Before that time another bill had been introduced in the

Reform bill in the House.

---

it was cheaper for the government at that time to buy bonds in the open market than to redeem them at par.

[1] See Mr. Finkelnburg's speech, *Congr. Globe*, 1871–72, pp. 2826–2829.

Senate, by the committee of that body on finance, which also lowered duties, but by no means in so incisive a manner as the House bill. The Senate bill simply proposed to reduce all the protective duties by ten per cent. When Ten per cent. reduction proposed. the ten per cent. reduction was first suggested, it was strongly opposed by the protected interests, whose representatives, it is hardly necessary to say, were present in full force. They were unwilling to yield even so small a diminution. When, however, the House bill, making much more radical changes, was brought forward with the sanction of a majority of the Committee on Ways and Means, they saw that an obstinate resistance to any change might lead to dangerous results. A change of policy was accordingly determined on. Mr. John L. Hayes, who has been for many years Secretary of the Wool-Manufacturers' Association, and was President of the Tariff Commission Policy of the protectionists. of 1882, was at that time in Washington as agent for the wool manufacturers. Mr. Hayes has given an account of the events at Washington in 1872, from which it appears that he was chiefly instrumental in bringing about the adoption of a more far-sighted policy by the protectionists.[1] Mr. Hayes believed it to be more easy to defeat the serious movement in favor of tariff reform by making some slight concessions than by unconditional

---

[1] See the speech which Mr. Hayes made, shortly after the close of the session of 1872, at a meeting of the wool manufacturers in Boston ; printed in the *Bulletin of the Wool Manufacturers*, vol. iii., pp. 283-290.

opposition. The woollen manufacturers were first induced to agree to this policy ; the Pennsylvania iron makers were next brought over to it; and finally, the whole weight of the protected interests was made to bear in the same direction. As a concession to the demand for reform, the general ten per cent. reduction was to be permitted. With this, however, was to be joined a sweeping reduction of the non-protective sources of revenue: the taxes on whiskey and tobacco were to be lowered, and the tea and coffee duties were to be entirely abolished.

This plan of action was successfully carried out. An act for abolishing the duties on tea and coffee was first passed.[1] This being disposed of, the general tax and tariff bill was taken up in the House. The Senate had already indicated its willingness to act in the manner desired by the protectionists. It had passed and sent to the House a bill making the general reduction of ten per cent., and nothing remained but to get the consent of the House. But this consent was not easily obtained. A large number of representatives were in favor of a more thorough and radical reform, and wished for the passage of the bill prepared by the Ways and Means Committee. But unfortunately the reform forces were divided, and only a part of them insisted on the Ways and Means bill. The remainder were willing to accept the ten per cent. reduction, which the protectionists yielded. On the other hand,

---

[1] The House had already passed, at the extra session in the spring of 1871, a bill for admitting tea and coffee free of duty. This bill was now taken up and passed by the Senate.

the protectionist members were united. Messrs. Kelley and Dawes led them, and succeeded in bringing their whole force to vote in favor of the horizontal reduction. The powerful influence of the Speaker, Mr. Blaine, was also on their side. They finally succeeded in having the original committee bill set aside, and in passing the bill for the ten per cent. reduction. Most of the revenue reformers in the end voted for it, believing it to be the utmost that could be obtained. It must be observed, how- Act of 1872. ever, to their credit, that the " horizontal " re- duction of the protective duties was not the only concession to the reform feeling that was made by the act of 1872. It also contained a number of minor but significant changes of duty. The duty on salt was reduced to one half the previous rates; for the feeling against the war-duty on salt, which very clearly resulted in putting so much money into the pockets of the Syracuse and Saginaw producers, was too strong to be resisted. The duty on coal was re- duced from $1.25 to 75 cents a ton. Some raw materials, of which hides and paper stock were alone of considerable importance, were admitted free of duty. The free list was also enlarged by putting on it a number of minor articles used by manufacturers. But the important change in the protective duties was the ten per cent. re- duction, which applied to all manufactures of cotton, wool, iron, steel, metals in general, paper, glass, and leather,—that is, to all the great protective industries.

It is worth while to dwell for a moment on the abolition

of the duties on tea and coffee. At the time much was

Removal of the tea and coffee duties.

said about this as an act for the benefit of the working man, to whom it was to give a " free breakfast-table." In fact, as it is hardly necessary to say, it was a distinctly protectionist measure. The loss of revenue which it caused would ordinarily have to be made good by imposing or retaining protective duties. As matters stood in 1872, it prevented at least a more complete reduction of the latter. The tea and coffee duties were among the simplest, most equable, and most productive sources of national revenue. As taxes, they were little felt by consumers. Most important to note, they yielded to the government every thing which they took out of the pockets of the tax-payers. This is their distinctive advantage over protective duties. A duty on imports, like every indirect tax, reaches the tax-payer in the shape of higher prices of the commodities which he consumes. When a duty is imposed on an article like tea or coffee, the whole increase of price to the consumer results in so much revenue to the government. But when a duty is imposed on an article like silks or linens, and results in the production (or in an increased production) of this article at home, the effect is different. Here also the commodity is increased in price to the consumer, and he is thereby taxed. So far as he uses imported articles, the increased price, as in the case of tea and coffee, is a tax paid to the government ; and as such it is not specially open to objection. But when the consumer buys and uses an article of this kind which is made at home, he must pay an increased price quite as much as when he buys the imported article. The increase of price, or tax, in such a case is not paid to the government, but to the home producer. It does not flow into the national revenue, and does not serve to pay for the performance of government functions. It flows into the pockets of a private individual. The private individual does not necessarily obtain, on account of this tax, exceptional profits in the production of the dutied, *i. e.*, protected, articles. It is true that in some cases of monopoly, as we shall have occasion to see, he may permanently make high profits. But in many cases he fails to do so. It may cost more, from inherent and natural causes, to make the protected article at home than it costs to make it abroad. In this case—the most frequent—the home producer gets a higher price in consequence of the duty; but he does not make correspondingly high profits. The tax on the consumer here represents simply the greater cost, the inherent natural disadvantage, of making the commodity at home. It represents a useless diversion of national industry. A commodity is made at home which can be more cheaply bought abroad; and nobody is benefited by the tax imposed on the consumer. All this is clear and familiar to every one who has grasped the fundamental principles of political economy; but so great a mass of untrue and sophistical writing is constantly put forth on the protective controversy, that the sound elementary principles cannot be too often repeated.

For these reasons import duties, where they must be levied, should be imposed primarily on articles like tea and coffee, óf which the domestic production will not be stimulated by the duties. In a government like ours, where the national revenue, by tradition and from the necessity of the case, is chiefly derived from import duties, these should be imposed primarily on non-protected commodities. At the most, it is only after such articles have yielded the revenue that they can reasonably and properly afford, that resort should be had to duties which operate for protection. But these principles have been often lost sight of in our tariff legislation.[1] In the legislation of the last twenty years they have been entirely disregarded. The removal of the tea and coffee duties is only one of a number of changes of the same kind. Step by step, in the various tariff acts which have been passed since the war, all the non-protective duties have been swept away, in order that the protective duties might be retained. Articles like cocoa, pepper, cinnamon, cloves, olives, the most natural and proper sources of revenue from import duties, have been admitted free of duty. The decisive step in this process was the tea and coffee act of 1872. There are at present none other than protective duties in our tariff. In recent years, when it has again brought in

---

[1] Even the tariffs of 1846 and 1857, which were supposed to be based on principles opposed to protection, admitted tea and coffee free of duty, while they imposed heavy duties on iron, cottons, woollens, etc.

an excessive revenue, those who oppose any diminution
of protection advocate, as a step analogous to the abolition of the tea and coffee duties, the removal of the internal taxes on tobacco, and even of those on spirits.
The object here is the same as it was in 1872,—to reduce
the revenue without touching the protective parts of the
tariff.

To return from this digression to the tariff act of 1872.
The free-traders were on the whole satisfied with it ; they
thought it a step in the right direction, and the beginning
of a process of reform. The protectionists, however,
believed that they had won a victory ; and, as events
proved, they were right.[1]

It is not within the purpose of this volume to discuss
the intrinsic merits of a " horizontal reduction," such as
was carried out in the act of 1872. Undoubtedly it is
a simple and indiscriminating method of approaching the
problem of tariff reform. The objections to it were
very prominently brought forward when Mr. Morrison,
during the session of 1883–84, proposed to take off ten per
cent. from the duties, in exactly the same way that the
tariff of 1872 had taken off ten per cent. It is certainly
curious that this method, when proposed by Mr. Morrison
in 1884, should be vehemently denounced by protectionists

---

[1] Mr. Hayes, in the speech already referred to, spoke of " the grand result of a tariff bill reducing duties fifty-three millions of dollars, and yet leaving the great industries almost intact. The present tariff (of 1872) was
made by our friends, in the interest of protection." And again : "A
reduction of over fifty millions of dollars, and yet taking only a shaving
off from the protection duties."

as crude, vicious, unscientific, and impractical, although, when proposed by Mr. Dawes in 1872, it received their earnest support. There is, however, one objection to such a plan which was hardly mentioned in connection with Mr. Morrison's bill, but was brought out very clearly by the experience of 1872. This is, that a horizontal reduction can very easily be revoked. The reduction made in 1872 was repealed with little difficulty in 1875. After the panic of 1873, imports greatly diminished, and

Ten per cent. reduction repealed in 1875. with them the customs revenue. No further thought of tax reduction was entertained ; and soon a need of increasing the revenue was felt. In 1875 Congress, as one means to that end, repealed the ten per cent. reduction, and put duties back to where they had been before 1872.[1] The repeal attracted comparatively little attention, and was

---

[1] It was far from necessary, for revenue purposes, to repeal the ten per cent. clause. Mr. Dawes (who advocated in 1875 the repeal of his own measure of 1872) attempted to show the need of raising the tariff by assuming that a fixed sum of $47,000,000 per year was necessary for the sinking-fund,—that the faith of the government was pledged to devoting this sum to the redemption of the debt. But it was very clearly shown that the government never had carried out the sinking-fund provision in any exact way. In some years it bought for the sinking fund much less than the one per cent of the debt which was supposed to be annually redeemed ; in other years (notably in 1869–73) it bought much more than this one per cent. The same policy has been followed in recent years. There can be little doubt that the need of providing for the sinking fund was used merely as an excuse for raising the duties. See Mr. Wood's remarks, *Congr. Record*, 1874–75, pp. 1187, 1188, and *cf.* Mr. Beck's speech, *ibid.*, pp.1401, 1402.

It may be noted that in 1875 President Grant and the Secretary of the Treasury recommended, and men like Senators Sherman and Schurz supported, a re-imposition of duties on tea and coffee as the best means of increasing the customs revenues.

carried without great opposition. If a detailed examination of the tariff had been made in 1872, and if duties had been reduced in that year carefully and with discrimination, it would have been much more difficult in 1875 to put them back to the old figures. If some of the duties which are of a particularly exorbitant or burdensome character had been individually reduced in 1872, public opinion would not easily have permitted the restitution of the old rates. But the general ten per cent. reduction, which touched none of the duties in detail, was repealed without attracting public attention. The old rates were restored; and the best opportunity which the country has had for a considerable modification of the protective system, slipped by without any permanent result.

Of the attempts at reform which were made between 1875 and 1883, little need be said. Mr. Morrison in 1876. and Mr. Wood in 1878, introduced tariff bills into the House. These bills were the occasion of more or less debate; but there was at no time any probability of their being enacted.[1] In 1879 the duty on quinine was abolished entirely,—a measure most beneficial and praiseworthy in itself, but not of any considerable importance in the economic history of the country.

Of the tariff act of 1883 we do not purpose speaking in

---

[1] Those who are interested in the details of these measures will find the bill of 1876 explained in Mr. Morrison's speech, in *Cong. Record*, 1875–1876, p. 3321. The bill of 1878 was similarly explained by Mr. Wood, *Cong. Record*, 1877–78, p. 2398. It was at one time supposed that Mr. Wood's bill might be passed by the House; but the enacting clause was struck out, after some debate, by a vote of 137 to 114.

this connection. It will be discussed in detail in the concluding pages.

We have now completed our account of the attempts to reform the tariff which were made between the close of the Civil War and the act of last year (1883). It is clear that the duties, as they were imposed in the act of 1864, were retained substantially without change during the whole of this period. The non-protective duties were indeed swept away. A few reductions of protective duties were made in the acts of 1870 and 1872; but the great mass of duties imposed on articles which are produced in this country were not touched. It is worth while to note some of the more important classes of goods on which the duties levied in 1864 remained in force, and to compare these duties with the rates of the Morrill tariff of 1861. The increase which was the result of the war will appear most plainly from such a comparison. In the appended table[1] it will be seen that the rates on books, chinaware, and pottery, cotton goods, linen, hemp, and jute goods, glass, gloves, bar- and hoop-iron, iron rails, steel, lead, paper, and silks, were increased by from ten to thirty per cent. during the war, and that the increase then made was maintained without the slightest change till 1883. That these great changes, at the time when they were made, were not intended or expected to be permanent, cannot be denied. An example like that of the duty on cotton goods shows plainly how the duties were

---

[1] See table III., Appendix.

fixed during the war according to the conditions of the time, and without expectation of their remaining indefinitely in force. The duty on the cheapest grade of cotton tissues had been in 1861 fixed at one cent per yard. During the war the price of cotton rose greatly, and with it the prices of cotton goods. Consequently it is not surprising to find the duty in 1864 to be five cents per yard on this grade of cottons. But shortly after the war, raw cotton fell nearly to its former price; and it does occasion surprise to find that the duty of five cents per yard should have been retained without change till 1883, and even in the act of 1883 retained at a figure much above that of 1861. The duty on cheap cottons happens not to have been particularly burdensome, since goods of this kind are made in this country as cheaply as they can be made abroad. But the retention of the war duty on them, even after it became exorbitantly high, is typical of the way in which duties were retained on other articles on which they were burdensome. Duties which had been imposed during the war, and which had then been made very high, either for reasons of revenue or because of circumstances such as led to the heavy rate on cottons, were retained unchanged after the war ceased. It would be untrue to say that protection did not exist before the great struggle began,—the tariff of 1861, was a distinctly protectionist measure; but it is clear that the extreme protectionist character of our tariff is an indirect and unexpected result of the Civil War.

CHAPTER III.

HOW DUTIES WERE RAISED ABOVE THE WAR RATES.

IN the preceding chapter it has been shown how the duties levied during the war failed to be reduced after its close. But in many cases not only has there been a failure to diminish the war rates, but an actual increase over them. We have already noted how the maintenance of the tariff of 1864 brought about gradually a feeling that such a system was a good thing in itself, and desirable as a permanent policy. This feeling, and the fact that Congress and the public had grown accustomed to heavy taxes and high rates, enabled many measures to become law which under normal circumstances would never have been submitted to. In the present chapter we are concerned with the not infrequent instances in which, in obedience to the demands of the protected interests, duties were raised over and above the point, already high, at which they were left when the war closed. The most striking instance of legislation of this kind is to be found in the wool and woollens act of 1867; a measure which is so characteristic of the complications of our tariff, of the remarkable height to which protection has been carried in it, and of the submission of Congress and the people to the demands of domestic manu- Wool and facturers that it deserves to be described woollen act in detail. Such a description is the more of 1867. desirable since the woollen schedule of our tariff is the one which imposes the heaviest and the least defensible burdens on consumers, and at the same time is the most difficult of comprehension for those who have nothing but the mere language of the statute to guide them.

In order to understand the complicated system that now exists, we must go back to the Morrill tariff act of 1861. In that act specific duties on wool were substituted for the *ad-valorem* rates of 1846 and 1857. The cheaper kinds of wool, costing eighteen cents or less per pound, were still admitted at the nominal rate of five per cent. But wool costing between eighteen and twenty-four cents per pound was charged three cents per pound; that costing more than twenty-four cents was charged nine cents per pound. The duties on woollens were increased correspondingly. An *ad-valorem* rate of twenty-five per cent. was levied on them; in addition they paid a specific duty of twelve cents for each pound of cloth. This specific duty was intended merely to compensate the manufacturers for the duty on wool, while the *ad-valorem* rate alone was to yield them any protection. This is the first appearance in our tariff history of the device of exact compensating duties. Compensation for duties on raw materials used by domestic producers had indeed been provided for in previous tariffs; but it was not until the passage of the Morrill act and of its successors that it came to be applied in this distinct manner. As the principle of compensation has been greatly extended since 1861, and is the key to the existing system of woollen duties, it may be well to explain it with some care.

It is evident that a duty on wool must normally cause the price of all wool that is imported to rise by the full extent of the duty. More-over, the duty presumably causes the wool grown at home, of the same grade as that imported, also to rise in price to the full extent of the tax. It is clear that, if foreign wool continues to be imported, such a rise in the price of domestic wool must take place; since wool will not be imported unless the price here is higher, by the amount of the duty, than the price abroad. It may happen, of course, that the tax will prove prohibitory, and that the importation of foreign wool will cease; in which case it is possible that the domestic wool is raised in price by some amount less than the duty, and even possible that it is not raised in price at all. Assuming for the present (and this assumption was made in arranging the compensating system) that domestic wool does rise in price, by the extent of the duty, as compared with foreign wool, it is evident that the American manufacturer, whether using foreign or domestic wool, is compelled to pay more for his raw material than his competitor abroad. This disadvantage it becomes necessary to offset by a compensating duty on foreign woollens. In 1861 the duty on wool of the kind chiefly used in this country (costing abroad between ten and twenty-four cents a pound) was three cents a pound. The compensating duty for this was made twelve cents a pound on the woollen cloth, which tacitly assumes that about four pounds of wool are used for each pound of cloth. This specific duty was intended to put the manufacturer in the same situation, as regards foreign competition, as if he got his wool free of duty. The separate *ad-valorem* duty of twenty-five per cent. was then added in order to give protection.

The compensating system was retained in the acts of 1862 and 1864. During the war, it is needless to say, the duties on wool and woollens were considerably raised. They were increased, and to some extent properly increased, to offset the internal taxes and the increased duties on dye-stuffs and other materials; and care was taken, in this as in other instances, that Wool and the increase in the tariff should be sufficient woollen du-and more than sufficient to prevent the do-ties of 1864. mestic producer from being unfairly handicapped by the internal taxes. In the final act of 1864 the duties on wool were as follows:

On wool costing 12 cents or less, a duty of 3 cents per pound.
   "   "   " between 12 and 24 cents, a duty of 6 cents per pound.
   "   "   "   " 24 and 32 cents, a duty of 10 cents per pound, plus ten per cent.
On wool costing more than 32 cents, a duty of 12 cents per pound, plus ten per cent.[1]

---

[1] Exactly how this duty on wool of ten per cent. on the value, in addition

The wool chiefly imported and chiefly used by our manufacturers was that of the second class, costing between twelve and twenty-four cents per pound, and paying a duty of six cents. The compensating duty on woollens was therefore raised in 1864 to twenty-four cents per pound of cloth. The *ad-valorem* (protective) duty on woollens had been raised to forty per cent.

During the war the production of wool and woollens had been greatly increased. The check to the manufacture of cotton goods, which resulted from the stoppage of the great source of supply of raw cotton, caused some increase in the demand for woollens. The government's need of large quantities of cloth for army use was also an important cause. After the war, a revolution was threatened. Cotton bade fair to take its former place among textile goods; the government no longer needed its woollens, and threw on the market the large stocks of army clothing which it had on hand. In the hope of warding off the imminent depression of their trade, the wool growers and manufacturers made an effort to obtain still further assistance from the government. A convention of wool growers and manufacturers was held in Syracuse, N. Y., in December, 1865. That both these classes of producers, as a body, understood and supported the views of this meeting, is not at all certain. The mass of wool growers undoubtedly knew

---

to the specific duty, came to be imposed, the writer has never seen satisfactorily explained. It probably came into the tariff in connection with the discriminating duty of ten per cent. which was imposed on goods imported in the vessels of nations that had no treaty of commerce with us.

nothing of it; they were represented chiefly by a few breeders of sheep. Among the manufacturers, many held aloof from it when its character became somewhat more plain. There is good evidence to show that the whole movement was the work of a few energetic manufacturers of New England, engaged chiefly in producing carpets and worsted goods, and of some prominent breeders of sheep.[1] The fact that the rates of duty, as arranged by the Syracuse convention, were especially advantageous to certain manufacturers—namely, those who made carpets, worsted goods, and blankets,—tends to support this view. On the surface, however, the movement appeared to be that of the growers and manufacturers united. The latter agreed to let the wool producers advance the duty on the raw material to any point they wished; they under-

---

[1] " This tariff (of 1867) was devised by carpet and blanket makers, who pretended to be ' The National Woollen Manufacturers' Association,' in combination with certain persons who raised fine bucks and wished to sell them at high prices, and who acted in the name of ' The National Wool-Growers' Association.' * * * A greater farce was never witnessed * * * Many who took part in the proceedings of 1866, finding that the Association [of Wool Manufacturers] was used for the convenience of special interests, have since withdrawn."—Harris, " Memorial," pp. 22, 23.

Mr. Harris says elsewhere : " The carpet interest was predominant [in the Wool Manufacturers' Association]. * * * The President was, and is now (1871), a large carpet manufacturer ; and the Secretary was a very talented and astute politician, from Washington, chosen by the influence of the President." And again : "The Association having spent considerable sums in various ways *peculiar to Washington* (the italics are Mr. Harris's) increased the annual tax on its members very largely ; and at the present time (1871) it is hopelessly in debt to its President."—"Protective Duties," pp. 9, 10 ; " The Tariff," p. 17. See also " Argument on Foreign Wool Tariff before Finance Committee of Senate," New York, 1871.

took, by means of the compensating device, to prevent any injury to themselves from the high duty on the wool they used. The tariff schedule which was the result of this combination was approved by the United States Revenue Commission.[1] It was made a part of the unsuccessful tariff bill of 1867, already referred to[2] ; and when that bill failed, it was made law by a separate act, to whose passage no particular objection seems to have been made. The whole course of events forms the most striking example—and such examples are numerous—of the manner in which, in recent tariff legislation, regard has been had exclusively to the producer. Here was an intricate and detailed scheme of duties, prepared by the producers of the articles to be protected, openly and avowedly with the intention of giving themselves aid ; and yet this scheme was accepted and enacted by the National Legislature without any appreciable change from the rates asked for, and without question as to its effect on the people at large.[3]

We turn now to examine this act of 1867, which remained in force till 1883, and in which no changes of

---

[1] Mr. Stephen Colwell, a disciple of the Carey protectionist school, was the member of this commission who had charge of the wool and woollens schedule. Mr. Wells, who was also a member of the commission, had nothing to do with this part of the tariff.

[2] *Ante*, p. 21.

[3] The proceedings of the Syracuse convention may be found in full in the volume of "Transactions of the Wool Manufacturers" ; also in " U. S. Revenue Report, 1866," pp. 360–419. Mr. Colwell's endorsement of the scheme is also in " U. S. Revenue Report, 1866," pp. 347-356. Mr. Wells, in his report of 1867, sharply criticised the act as passed.

great importance are made by the existing tariff. In this examination we will follow the statement published in 1866, in explanation of the new schedule, by the Executive Committee of the National Association of Wool Manufacturers.[1]   To begin with, the duties Act of 1867. on wool were arranged on a new plan.   Wool Duty on wool. was divided into three classes: carpet, clothing, and combing wool.[2]   The first class, carpet wool, corresponded to the cheap wools of the tariff of 1864.   The duty was three cents a pound if it cost twelve cents or less, and six cents a pound if it cost more than twelve cents.   The other two classes, of clothing and combing wools, are the grades chiefly grown in this country, and therefore are most important to note in connection with the protective controversy.   The duties on these were the same for both classes.   Clothing and combing wools alike were made to pay as follows:

Value 32 cents or less, a duty of 10 cents per pound and 11 per cent. *ad valorem.*

Value more than 32 cents, a duty of 12 cents per pound and 10 per cent. *ad valorem.*[3]

---

[1] See " Statement of the Executive Committee of the Wool Manufacturers Association to the U. S. Revenue Commisson," printed in " Transactions," as above ; also printed in " Revenue Report for 1866," pp. 441–460.

[2] Clothing wool is of comparatively short fibre ; it is *carded* as a preparation for spinning ; it is used for making cloths, cassimeres, and the other common woollen fabrics.   Combing wool is of longer fibre ; it is *combed* in a combing machine as a preparation for spinning ; and it is used in making worsted goods, and other soft and pliable fabrics.

[3] Here again we have the rather absurd combination of specific and *ad-valorem* duties on wool.   In the act of 1867, there is the further complication

Comparing these figures with the rates of 1864, one would not, at first sight, note any great change.   In 1864, wool costing between twenty-four and thirty-two cents had been charged ten cents per pound plus ten per cent. *ad valorem;* and wool costing more than thirty-two cents had paid twelve cents a pound plus ten per cent.   These seem to be almost exactly the rates of 1867.   But in fact, by the change in classification, a very considerable increase in the duty was brought about.   In 1867 *all* wool costing less than thirty-two cents was made to pay the duty of ten cents per pound and eleven per cent.   In 1864 wool cost-ing (abroad) between eighteen and twenty-four cents had been charged only six cents per pound.   This is the class of wool chiefly grown in the United States, and chiefly imported hither; and it was charged in 1867 with the duty of ten cents and eleven per cent.   With the *ad-valorem* addition, the duty of 1867 amounted to eleven and a half or twelve cents a pound, or about double the duty of 1864.   The consequence was that in reality the duty on that grade of wool which is chiefly used in this country was nearly doubled by the act of 1867 ; and the increase was concealed under a change in classification. The duty on clothing and combing wools, as fixed in

---

that the *ad-valorem duty* is in the one case ten per cent., in the other eleven per cent.   This difference resulted by accident, as the writer has been in-formed, from the need of complying technically with certain parliamentary rules of the House.   It is hardly necessary to say that this mixture of specific and *ad-valorem* duties on wool has no connection with the compensating system.   The compensating scheme accounts only for the two kinds of duties on *woollen goods.*

1867, has been on the average more than fifty per cent. on the value abroad.

The duty on wool being fixed in this way, that on woollens was arranged on the following plan. It was calculated that four pounds of wool (unwashed) were needed to produce *The duty on woollen cloths.* a pound of cloth. The duty on wool, as has been explained, amounted to about eleven and one half cents a pound, taking the specific and *ad-valorem* duty together. Each of the four pounds of wool used in making a pound of cloth, paid, if imported, a duty of four times eleven and one half cents, or forty-six cents. If home, grown wool was used, the price of this, it was assumed, was equally raised by the duty. The manufacturer in either case paid, for the wool used in making a pound of cloth, forty-six cents more than his foreign competitor. For this disadvantage he must be compensated. Moreover, the manufacturer in the United States, in 1867, paid duties on drugs, dye-stuffs, oils, etc., estimated to amount to two and one half cents per pound of cloth. For this also he must be compensated. In addition he must have interest on the duties advanced by him; for between the time when he paid the duties on the wool and other materials, and the time when he was reimbursed by the sale of his cloth, he had so much money locked up. Add interest for, say six months, and we get the final total of the duty necessary to compensate the manufacturer for what he has to pay on his raw materials. The account stands :

Duty on 4 pounds of wool at 11½ cents	.	.	.			46	cents
" " oils, dye-stuffs, etc.	.	.	.	.	.	2½	"
Interest	.	.	.	.	.	.	.	4½	"

Total	.	.	.	.	53	"

Congress did not accept the exact figure set by the woollen makers. It made the compensating duty fifty cents per pound of cloth instead of fifty-three; but this change was evidently of no material importance. The woollen manufacturers got substantially all that they wanted. It will be remembered that in 1864 the compensating specific duty on cloth had been only twenty-four cents per pound.

The *ad-valorem* duty was fixed at thirty-five per cent. The woollen manufacturers said they wanted a "net effective protection" of only twenty-five per cent.[1] This does not seem immoderate. But ten per cent *ad-valorem* was supposed to be necessary to compensate for the internal taxes, which were still imposed in 1867, though abolished very soon after. This ten per cent., added to the desired protection of twenty-five per cent, brought the *ad-valorem*

---

[1] "All manufactures composed wholly or in part of wool or worsted shall be subjected to a duty which shall be equal to twenty-five per cent. net ; *that is,* twenty-five per cent. after reimbursing the amount paid on account of wool, dye-stuffs, and other imported materials, and also the amount paid for the internal revenue tax imposed on manufactures and on the supplies and materials used therefor." Joint Report of Wool Manufacturers and Wool Growers, "Revenue Report, for 1866," p. 430; also in "Transactions." The Executive Committee of the Wool Manufacturers' Association said, in 1866 : "Independently of considerations demanding a duty on wool, the wool manufacturers would prefer the total abolition of specific duties, provided they could have all their raw material free, and an actual net protection of twenty-five per cent." Harris, "Memorial," p. 9.

rate to thirty-five per cent. The final duty on woollen cloth was therefore fifty cents per pound and thirty-five per cent. *ad valorem:* of which the fifty cents was compensation for duties on raw materials; ten per cent. was compensation for internal tax; and of the whole accumulated mass only twenty-five per cent. was supposed to give protection to the manufacturer.

This duty was levied on woollen cloths, woollen shawls, and manufactures of wool not otherwise provided for— categories which include most of the woollen goods made in this country. On other classes of goods the same system was followed. An *ad-valorem* duty of thirty-five per cent. was imposed in all cases; twenty-five per cent. being intended to be protection, and ten per cent. compensation for internal taxes. Duty on flannels, carpets, dress goods, etc. The specific duty varied with different goods, but in all cases was supposed merely to offset the import duties on wool and other supplies. For instance, on flannels, blankets, and similar goods, the specific duty varied from fifty cents a pound to twenty cents, being made to decrease on the cheaper qualities of goods, as less wool, or cheaper wool, was used in making a pound of flannel or blanket. The duties on knit goods were the same as those on blankets. On carpets the system was applied with some modification. The specific duty was levied here *by the square yard*, and not by the pound. A calculation was made of the quantity of wool, linen, yarn, dye-stuffs, and other imported articles used for each yard of carpet; the total duties paid on these materials, with interest added as in the case of cloth, gave the compensating duty per yard of carpet. On this basis, for instance, the specific duty on Brussels carpets was made forty-four cents per yard (the manufacturers had asked for a duty of forty-eight cents); the *ad-valorem* duty of thirty-five per cent. being of course also imposed. In the same way the specific duty on dress goods for women's and children's wear was made from six to eight cents per yard, according to quality. It is evident that the task of making the specific duty exactly compensate for the duties on wool was most complicated in these cases, and that any excess of compensation would here be most difficult of discovery for those not very familiar with the details of the manufacture. As a matter of fact, it is precisely in these schedules of the woollens act that, as we shall see, the " compensating " system was used as a means of securing a high degree of protection for the manufacturer.

These duties, *ad valorem* and specific taken together, have been from fifty to one hundred per cent., and even more, on the cost of the goods. On cloths generally they have been from sixty to seventy per cent. on the value. On blankets and flannels they have been from eighty to one hundred per cent., and have been entirely prohibitory of importation. On dress goods they have been from sixty to seventy per cent.; on Brussels carpets again from sixty to seventy per cent.; and on ingrain carpets from fifty to fifty-five per cent. Yet a net protection of twenty-five per cent. is all that the manufacturers asked for and were intended to have; and the question naturally presents itself, did they not in fact get more than twenty-five per cent.?

The first conclusion that can be drawn from this explanation of the woollens duties is that there was at all events no good reason for the permanent retention of the *ad-valorem* rate of thirty-five per cent. Of that rate ten per cent. was in all cases meant to compensate for the internal taxes. These disappeared entirely within a year or two after the woollens act was passed. Yet the *ad-valorem* rate on woollens remained at thirty-five per cent. without change from 1867 to 1883. In the present tariff, that of 1883, it still is thirty-five per cent. in most cases; and where it has been changed at all, it has even been raised to forty per cent. There is no more striking illustration of the way in which duties which were imposed in order to offset the internal taxes of the war period, have been retained and have become permanent parts of our tariff system, although the original excuse for their imposition has entirely ceased to exist.

It may seem that the retention of the specific duties on woollens was justified, since the duties on wool were not changed. It is true that the duties on dye-stuffs, drugs, and such articles have been abolished or greatly reduced since 1867; but these played no great part in the determina-

tion of the specific duty.   The duties on wool were
not changed till the passage of the act of 1883.   There
are, however, other grounds for criticising the specific
duties on woollens, which have been in fact not merely
compensating, but have added, in most cases, a considerable degree of protection to the " net " twenty-five per
cent. which the act of 1867 was supposed to give the
manfacturers.

The compensating duties, as we have seen, were based
on two assumptions: first, that the price of wool, whether
foreign or domestic, was increased by the full extent of
the duty ; second, that four pounds of wool were used in
making a pound of cloth.   The first assumption, however,
holds good only to a very limited extent.   A protective
duty does not necessarily cause the price of the protected
article to rise by the full extent of the duty.   It may be
prohibitory; the importation of the foreign article may
entirely cease ; and the domestic article, while its price is
raised to some extent, may yet be dearer by an amount less
than the duty.   This is what has happened with regard to
most grades of wool.   The commoner grades of wool are
raised in this country with comparative ease.   The duty
on them is prohibitory, and their importation has ceased.
Their price, though higher than that of similar wools
abroad, is not higher by the full extent of the duty.   It is
true that the importation of finer grades of clothing and
combing wools continues ; and it is possible that the wools
of Ohio, Michigan, and other States east of the Mississippi

are higher in price, by the full amount of the duty, than similar wools abroad. Even this is not certain ; for the wools which continue to be imported are not of precisely the same class as the Ohio and Michigan wools. As a rule, the importations are for exceptional and peculiar purposes, and do not replace or compete with domestic wools. At all events, it is certain that the great mass of wools grown in this country are entirely shielded from foreign competition. Their price is raised above the foreign price of similar material ; but raised only by some amount less than the duty. The manufacturer, however, gets a compensating duty in all cases as if his material were dearer, by the full extent of the duty, than that of his foreign competitor. The bulk of the wool used by American manufacturers does not show the full effect of the tariff, and the manufacturers clearly obtain, in the specific duty, more compensation than the higher price of their wool calls for. The result is that this duty, instead of merely preventing the domestic producer from being put at a disadvantage, yields him in most cases a considerable degree of protection, over and above that given by the *ad-valorem* duty.[1]

There is another way in which the compensating duty is excessive. A very large quantity of woollen goods are

---

[1] See the instructive remarks of Mr. John L. Hayes, in *Bulletin Wool Manufacturers* vol. xiii. pp. 98–108. *Cf.* " Tariff Comm. Report," pp. 1782–1785. The production and importation of wool in different parts of the country for a series of years are given in some detail in " Tariff Comm. Report," pp. 2435, 2436.

not made entirely of wool. Cotton, shoddy, and other substitutes are in no inconsiderable part the materials of the clothes worn by the mass of the people. In these goods very much less than four pounds of wool is used in making a pound of cloth, and the specific duty again yields to the manufacturer a large degree of protection.

The second assumption of the compensating system. that four pounds of wool are used in making a pound of cloth, is also open to criticism. The goods in which cotton and shoddy are used clearly do not require so much wool. But it is probable that even with goods made entirely of wool, the calculation of four pounds of unwashed wool for each pound of cloth is very liberal. Wool, unwashed, shrinks very much in the cleaning and scouring which it must receive before it is fit for use ; and the loss by wear and waste in the processes of manufacture is also considerable. The shrinkage in scouring is subject to no definite rule. In some cases wool loses only forty per cent. of its weight in the process, in others as much as seventy-five per cent. The shrinkage in scouring on American wools is rarely more than sixty per cent ; and if to this is added a further loss of twenty-five per cent. in manufacture, there will be needed for a pound of cloth no more than three and one third pounds of wool.'

---

[1] See, as to the loss of wool in scouring, *Quarterly Report Bureau of Statistics,* for quarter ending June 30, 1884, pp. 563–565 ; Harris, " Memorial," p. 11 ; Schoenhof, " Wool and Woollens," p. 10 ; *Bulletin Wool Mf.,* vol. xiii., p. 8. The least loss I have found mentioned is twenty-five per cent. (coarse Ohio), and the highest seventy per cent. (Buenos Ayres wool). Ordinary

With the great majority of goods made in this country, the shrinkage and the loss in manufacture do not amount to more than this. The calculation of four for one is for most American goods a liberal one ; and it is evident that the compensating duty, based on this liberal calculation, yields a degree of protection in the same way that it does on goods that contain cotton or shoddy. On the other hand, there are some grades of imported wool on which the shrinkage and loss in manufacture are so great that the compensating duty is not excessive. Some grades of Australian wool, which are imported for manufacturing fine goods and worsteds, are subject to exceptional shrinkage and to exceptional waste in the process of manufacture. Of this class of wool four pounds, and sometimes a little more, are apt to be used for a pound of cloth.[1] In such cases the compensating duty evidently

---

American wool loses between fifty and sixty per cent. in scouring. The loss in weight in manufacturing varies much with the processes, but with care will not exceed twenty-five per cent. With most goods it is less.

If the loss in scouring 100 lbs. of wool is sixty per
    cent., there remain . . . . . 40 lbs. scoured wool.
Deduct twenty-five per cent. for loss in manufacture 10 lbs.

                    Leaves . . 30 lbs. of cloth,
or 1 lb. of cloth for 3⅓ lbs. of wool.
If the loss in scouring 100 lbs. of wool is sixty-five
    per cent. there remain . . . . 35 lbs. scoured wool.
Deduct twenty-five per cent. for loss in manufacture
. . . . 8¾ lbs.

                    Leaves. . . 26¼ lbs. of cloth,
or 1 lb. cloth for not quite 4 lbs. of wool.

[1] See the instances given by Mr. Hayes in *Wool Manufacturers' Bulletin*, vol. xii., pp. 4–9. These all refer to Australian wool, which, as Mr. Hayes says elsewhere (*ibid.*, p. 107), is imported in comparatively small quantities for exceptional purposes.

may fail to counterbalance entirely the disadvantage under which the manufacturer labors in the higher price of his raw material; for the wool, being imported into this country, and paying the duty, must be higher in price by the full amount of the duty than the same wool used by the foreign producer. In other words, there are cases where the specific duty is not sufficient to offset the duty on the raw material. It is probable that this fact explains, in part at least, the regular importation of certain dress goods and finer grades of cloths, which continue to come into the country from abroad in face of the very heavy duty. But such cases are exceptional. For most goods made in the United States the compensating duty on the four to one basis is excessive.

One other provision in the act of 1867 may be pointed out, which bears on the calculation of four pounds of wool to one pound of cloth, and at the same time illustrates the spirit in which the act was prepared. It has already been said that the duty on wool is laid on *unwashed* wool; and the compensating duty is fixed on the calculation that it requires four pounds of unwashed wool to make a pound of cloth. The act of 1867 provided that clothing wool, if washed, should pay double duty, and if scoured, treble duty. Similarly combing wool and carpet wool were made to pay treble duty if scoured. But no provision whatever was made as to combing and carpet wools if *washed;* they were admitted at the same rate of duty whether washed or unwashed. This amounted practically to a lowering of the duty on them. The same wool which would weigh, if unwashed, one and one half pounds, and would be charged with a duty of twenty cents, would weigh, if washed, only about a pound, and would pay a duty of only thirteen cents. The result was that combing and carpet wool was advantageously imported in a washed condition, and the duty was in effect appreciably below the rate on unwashed wool. Yet the compensating duty on carpets, worsteds, and all goods made from these wools was arranged as in the case of cloths, as if the full rate on unwashed wool were levied. The manufacturer got the full compensating rate on his product, though he did not pay the full duty on his wool. It is a well-known fact that this anomaly in the act of 1867 was due chiefly to a prominent manufacturer of New England, whose business, as a consequence, was made exceedingly profitable during the years immediately succeeding the passage of the act.[1]

If, as we have seen the case to be, the compensating duty was very liberal in the case of ordinary woollen cloth, where the calculations on which it was founded can be checked with comparative ease, it is to be expected

---

[1] The act of 1883 maintains without change the admission of washed combing wool at the same rates of unwashed. The great profits which this state of things enabled certain worsted manufacturers to make in the first instance, have been brought down by the force of domestic competition ; and a considerable industry has grown up on the basis of the easy admission of washed wool. It would, therefore, hardly be wise to revert from it at the present time. But its insertion in the original act is very characteristic of the spirit in which the compensating scheme was devised.

that other schedules, where a check is more difficult to apply, will also contain excessive compensation. The specific duty on carpets is levied by the yard; that on Brussels carpets, for instance, was forty-four cents a square yard. Similarly the specific duty on dress-goods was levied by the square yard. That on blankets, flannels, worsteds, yarns, etc., was fixed by the pound, but was made to vary from twenty to fifty cents a pound, according to the value of the goods. The last-mentioned goods, for instance, paid a duty of twenty cents a pound if worth forty cents or less a pound; a duty of thirty cents if worth between forty and sixty cents; and so on. In every case, of course, the *ad-valorem* (nominally protective) rate of thirty-five per cent. was added to the specific duties. It is evidently a very complex problem whether these "compensating" duties represent the exact sum necessary to offset the increased price of materials due to the tariff rates on wool, hemp, dye-stuffs, and other dutiable articles used by manufacturers. We have seen that the movement that resulted in the passage of the act of 1867 was brought about chiefly by the manufacturers of carpets and worsteds. These men adjusted the specific duties, and alone could know with how great accuracy they attained their object of compensation. In some instances it was confessed that there was more than compensation in their scheme; this was admitted to be the case with blankets and dress-goods. On all goods it is not to be doubted that a liberal allowance was made in favor of the manufacturers, and that the specific rates gave them a great amount of pure and simple protection.

The truth is that the wool and woollens schedule, as it was enacted in 1867, and as it now remains in force with the modifications made in 1883, is a great sham. Nominally, it makes an exact division between protective and compensating duties; and nominally, it limits the protection for the manufacturer to twenty-five (now thirty-five) per cent. As a matter of fact, no one can tell how much of the different duties is protective, and how much merely compensating. So complicated is the schedule, and so varying are the conditions of trade and manufacture, that the domestic manufacturer himself finds it difficult to say exactly how great a degree of encouragement the government gives him. In some exceptional cases the effectual protection may be less than the twenty-five (now thirty-five) per cent. which the tariff is supposed to yield. In the great majority of cases it is very much more than this, and was meant to be more. The whole cumbrous and intricate system,—of *ad-valorem* and specific duties, of duties varying according to the weight and the value and the square yard,—was adopted, it is safe to say, simply because it concealed the degree of protection which in fact the act of 1867 gave. Duties that plainly and palpably levied taxes of 60, 80, and 100 per cent. would hardly have been suffered by public opinion or enacted by the legislature. Probably few members of Congress under-

The woollens act a heavy protective measure in disguise.

stood the real nature and bearing of the scheme; and no attempt was made to check the calculations of the woollen manufacturers, or to see whether, intentionally or by accident, abuses might not have crept into their proposals.

The most remarkable fact in the history of this piece of legislation was its failure to secure the object which its supporters had in mind. Notwithstanding the very great degree of protection which the manufacturers got, the production of woollen goods proved to be one of the most unsatisfactory and unprofitable of manufacturing occupations. As a rule, a strong protective measure causes domestic producers to obtain, at least for a time, high profits; though under the ordinary circumstances of free competition, profits are sooner or later brought down to the normal level. But in the woollen manufacture even this temporary gain was not secured by the home producers after the act of 1867. A few branches, such as the production of carpets, of blankets, of certain worsted goods, were highly profitable for some years. These were the branches, it will be remembered, in which the compensating duties were most excessive, and the prominent manufacturers engaged in them had done most to secure the passage of the act of 1867. Profits in these branches were in course of time brought down to the usual level, and in many instances below the usual level, by the increase of domestic production and domestic competition.

Manu-
facturers not
benefited
by the act.

The manufacture of the great mass of woollen goods, however, was depressed and unprofitable during the years immediately following the act, notwithstanding the speculative activity and seeming prosperity of that time.[1] It has sometimes been said that this was the effect of the act itself ; but other causes, such as the cessation of the the war demand and the increasing use of worsted goods in place of woollen goods, probably suffice to account for the unprosperous state of affairs. It has also been said that the lack of diversity in the woollen manufacture of the United States can be traced to those provisions in the act of 1867 by which particularly high protection was given on the common and cheaper goods ; the more so since the high duty on wool has tended to hamper the manufacturer in the choice of his material. No doubt it is true that at present the majority of finer woollen goods are imported, and the manufacture in this country is confined mainly to cheaper grades. The situation is not essentially different from that which we have already described as existing before 1860.[2] But here again too much is ascribed, for good or evil, to the tariff. The

---

[1] See an instructive article, by a manufacturer, in " Bulletin Nat. Assoc. Wool Mf.," vol. III , p. 354 (1872). " There is one thing that all who are interested in the manufacture will agree to, that for the last five years [from 1867 to 1872) the business in the aggregate has been depressed, that the profits made during the war have been exhausted mainly, and that it has been extremely difficult during all this time to buy wool and mannfacture it into goods and get a new dollar for an old one."—*Cf.* Mr. Harris' pamphlets, cited above.

[2] See above, p. 147.

limited range of the woollen manufacturer is probably due to deeper causes ; in part to the adaptability of the domestic wool for making the woollen goods which form the staples of the American manufacture, in part to the fact that the methods and machinery for those goods are fitted to our economic conditions.   The causes, in fact, are probably analogous to those which have confined the cotton manufacture within a limited range.   But, on the other hand, it is clear that the act of 1867 has not been successful as a protective measure ; it has not stimulated the woollen industry to any noticeable degree, nor has it greatly affected the character or extent of the imports. So far as the wool-growers are concerned, it has not prevented the price of wool from declining in the United States, in sympathy with the decline elsewhere ; nor has it prevented the shifting of wool-growing from the heart of the country to the western plains, where wool is raised under conditions like those of Australia and the Argentine Republic.   The manufacture probably would have been, on the whole and in the long run, more satisfactory to those engaged in it if they had had free wool and if woollens had been charged with no more than the protection of 25 per cent. which the act of 1867 was supposed to give.[1]   Some establishments, no doubt, have arisen which could not continue under such a system, and for these temporary provisions should be made if the present duties are swept away.

---

[1] This statement does not lack the authority of men of practical experience ; I may mention Mr. Rowland Hazard, of Providence, R. I., a large manu-

The woollens act of 1867 has been discussed somewhat at length because it is the most striking illustration of the manner in which protective duties were advanced after the war at the request of domestic producers. There are not a few other cases in which an increase of duties beyond the level reached during the war was made. After the woollens act, perhaps the most remarkable is the copper act of 1869. Before that year the duty on copper ore had been five per cent., that on copper in bars and ingots had been two and a half cents per pound. Under the very low duty on copper ore a large industry had grown up in Boston and Baltimore. Ore was imported from Chili, and was smelted and refined in these cities. But during the years immediately preceding 1869 the great copper mines of Lake Superior had begun to be worked on a considerable scale. These mines are probably the richest sources of copper in the world, and under normal circum-

Copper act of 1869.

---

facturer, who has kindly permitted the use of his name as sanctioning the text on this point.

It is not part of the object of this volume to discuss in detail the economic effect of the duties on wool and woollens. The reader is referred to a discussion of the original scheme in Mr. Wells's "Report of 1866–67," pp. 50–60; also to Mr. Wells's "Report for 1869–70," pp. xcii–cv.; Wells, "Wool and the Tariff" (1873); Harris, "Memorial to Committee on Ways and Means" (1872); Schoenhof, "Wool and Woolens" (1883); R. Hazard, "Address before the Washington County Agr. Society" (1884). On the other side, see *Bulletin Wool Manufacturers*, vol. ii., pp. 19–34, in reply to Wells's remarks in 1870; "Examination of Statements in the Report of the Revenue Commissioner," House Rep., 41st Congress, 2d session, Report No. 72 (1869–70); *Bulletin Wool Mfr.*, vol, xiii., p. 1–13; "Tariff Comm. Report," pp. 2240–47, 2411–2440.

stances would supply the United States with this metal
more cheaply and abundantly than any other country;
yet through our tariff policy these very mines have
caused us for many years to pay more for our copper
than any other country. The increased production from
these mines, with other circumstances, had caused copper
to fall in price in 1867 and 1868; and their owners came
before Congress and asked for an increase of duties. Copper ore was to pay three cents for each pound of pure copper, equal to twenty-five or thirty per cent., in place of the
previous duty of five per cent.; and ingot copper was to
pay five cents per pound, instead of two and a half cents.
The bill making these changes was passed by both houses.
President Johnson refused to sign it, and sent in a veto
message, which bore marks of having been composed by
other hands than his own. But the President was then perhaps the most unpopular man in the country; Congress
had got a habit of overriding his vetoes, and the copper bill
was passed in both Houses by the necessary two-thirds
vote, and became law.[1]   A more open use of legislation

---

[1] The veto message is in *Congress. Record*, 1868–69, p 1460. It was
written by Mr. David A. Wells, as that gentleman has informed the writer.
The character of the bill was made clear enough in the course of the debate,
at well as by the veto message. See Brooks's speech, *ibid.*, p. 1462.   The
manner in which this bill, and others of the same kind, were carried through
Congress is illustrated by some almost naive remarks of Mr. Frelinghuysen :
" My sympathies are with this bill, as they always are for any tariff bill.   I
confess, however, that I do not like this system of legislation, picking out
first wool, then copper, then other articles, and leaving the general manufacturing interests without that protection to which they are entitled, and
thus dividing the strength which those great interests ought to have.   But

for the benefit of private individuals has probably never been made. The effect of the act was, in the first place, to destroy the smelting establishments which had treated the Chilian ores. In the second place, it enabled the copper producers at home to combine and to settle the price of their product without being checked by any possible foreign competition. It is a well-known fact that the mining companies of Lake Superior, which controlled until within a year or two almost the entire production of copper in the United States, have maintained for many years a combination for fixing the price of copper. Their price has been steadily higher than the price of copper abroad; and when they have found it impossible to dispose of all their product at home at the combination price, large quantities have been sent abroad and sold there at lower prices, in order to relieve the home market. Several of these companies have paid for a series of years enormous profits—profits due in part, no doubt, to the unsurpassed richness of their mines, but in part also to the copper act of 1869.[1]

Still another instance of the increase of duties since the war is to be found in the case of steel rails. Before 1870 steel rails had been charged with duty under the head of

still, if a bill is introduced which gives protection to copper, trusting to the magnanimity of the Representatives from the West who have wool and copper protected, I should probably vote for the bill."—*Ibid.*, p. 161.

[1] On the effect of the copper act, see Mr. Wells's Essay, already referred to, in the Cobden Club series, pp. 518–521 *Cf.* the "Report of the Tariff Comm.," pp. 2554–2577. See also Appendix, V., where the total production of copper in each year, prices at home and abroad, etc., are given.

"manufacturers of steel not otherwise provided for," and
Steel rails, as such had paid forty-five per cent. The
1870. tariff act of 1870 changed this to a specific
duty of 1¼ cents per pound, or $28 per gross ton.
At the time, the change caused an increase, but no
very great increase, in the duty. The Bessemer process
of making steel had hardly begun to be used in 1870,
and the price of steel rails at that time in England
was about $50 per ton. The *ad-valorem* rate of forty-
five per cent., calculated on this price, would make the
duty $22.50 per ton, or not very much less than the duty
of $28 per ton imposed by the act of 1870. Between
1870 and 1873, the price of steel rails advanced in England, and the specific duty of $28 imposed in the former
year was not higher than the *ad-valorem* rate of forty-five
per cent. would have been. But after 1873 the prices of
Bessemer steel and of steel rails steadily went down. As
they did so, the specific duty became heavier in proportion to the price. By 1877 the average price of steel rails
in England was only a little over $31 per ton; and since
1877 the English price has not on the average been so
high as $28 per ton. The duty of $28, which this country
imposed, has therefore been equivalent to more than one
hundred per cent on the foreign price. The result of this
exorbitant duty was an enormous gain to the producers of
steel rails in the United States. The patent for the use of
the Bessemer process was owned by a comparatively small
number of companies; and these companies, aided by a

patent at home and protected by an enormous duty against foreign competitors, were enabled for a time to obtain exceedingly high prices for steel rails. During the great demand for railroad materials which began on the revival of business in 1879, and continued for several years thereafter, the prices of steel rails were advanced so high that English rails were imported into this country even though paying the duty of one hundred per cent. During this time the price in England was on the average in 1880 about $36 per ton, and in 1881 about $31 per ton. In this country during the same years the price averaged $67 and $61 per ton. That is, consumers in this country were compelled to pay twice as much for steel rails as they paid in England. Any thing which increases the cost of railroad-building tends to increase the cost of transportation; and a tax of this kind eventually comes out of the pockets of the people in the shape of higher railroad-charges for carrying freight and passengers. The domestic producers of steel rails secured enormous profits, of one hundred per cent. and more on their capital, during these years. These profits, as is always the case, caused a great extension of production. The men who had made so much money out of Bessemer steel in 1879–81 put this money very largely into establishments for making more steel. New works were erected in all parts of the country. At the same time the demand fell off, in consequence of the check to railroad-building; and the increased supply, joined to the small demand, caused prices here to fall almost to the English rates. But during the years of speculation and railroad-building the tariff had yielded great gains to makers of steel rails; and popular feeling against this state of things was so strong that in 1883 Congress felt compelled, as we shall see, to make a considerable reduction in the duty.[1]

Still another case, and one which bears some resemMarble, 1864 blance to the woollen act of 1867, is to be and 1870. found in the change of the duty on marble, which was made in 1870. The duty on marble had been put in 1864 at fifty cents per cubic foot, and twenty per cent. in addition. This, it may be remarked, is one of the not infrequent cases in which our tariff has imposed, and still imposes, both *ad-valorem* and specific duties on the same article. No compensating principle, such as is found in the woollen schedule, explains most of these mixed duties; and it is hard to find any good reason for retaining them, and giving the customs authorities the task of assessing the duty both on value of the article and on its weight or measure. The cause of their retention, there can be little doubt, is that they serve to conceal the real extent of the duties imposed. The duty on marble, for instance, had been thirty per cent. in 1861, and had been raised to forty per

---

[1] The effect of the steel-rail duty is discussed more in detail in Mr. J. Schoenhof's "Destructive Influence of the Tariff," ch. vii. On the profits made by the manufacturers, see Mr. A. S. Hewitt's speech in Congress, May, 16, 1882, *Congress. Record,* pp. 3980–83 ; also printed separately. *Cf. infra,* p. 94, and figures of production, prices, etc. in Appendix, VI.

cent. in 1862. The mixed duty put on in 1864 was equivalent to eighty per cent. and more.[1] A direct increase of the duty from forty to eighty per cent. would hardly have been ventured on; but the adoption of the mixed duty veiled the change which was in fact made. One would have supposed that this rate of eighty per cent. would have sufficed even for the most ardent supporter of home industries; but in 1870 a still further increase was brought about. It was then enacted that marble sawed into slabs of a thickness of two inches or less should pay twenty-five cents for each superficial square foot, and thirty per cent. in addition; slabs between two and three inches thick should pay thirty-five cents per square foot, and thirty per cent.; slabs between three and four inches thick should pay forty-five cents per square foot, and thirty per cent.; and so on in proportion. Marble more than six inches thick paid at the old rate of fifty cents per cubic foot, and twenty per cent. It is evident that the change made in the duty on marble in slabs caused a great increase. The duty on the thinnest slabs (two inches or less in thickness) became $1.50 per cubic foot, and thirty per cent. in addition; this same

---

[1] The duty of 1864 was fixed, as Mr. Morrill then explained, in accordance with an arrangement made between the importing merchants and " the gentlemen in Washington in the marble-quarry interest." The latter were Mr. Morrill's constituents. It did not seem to occur to that gentleman that the persons who were to pay for the marble should be regarded at all. Originally Mr. Morrill had even proposed a duty of seventy-five cents per cubic yard, with twenty per cent. in addition. See *Congr. Globe*, 1863-64, pp. 2746-2747.

marble had hitherto been admitted at fifty cents per cubic foot, and twenty per cent. The new rates of 1870 have been equivalent to between 100 and 150 per cent. on the value, and have been practically prohibitive. The effect of the marble duty and of the change made in it in 1870 can be understood only by those who know the circumstances under which marble is produced and imported in this country. The only marble imported, and that which alone is affected by the duty, is fine marble used for ornamental purposes in mantel-pieces, furniture, gravestones, etc. Such marble comes into use very largely in the shape of slabs of a few inches in thickness. The marble is imported, notwithstanding the heavy duty, from Italy, whence it is brought cheaply by ships that have taken out grain and other bulky cargoes. It is produced in the United States in a single district in Vermont. The owners of the marble quarries in this district have their product raised in price almost to the extent of the duty of eighty or 150 per cent. The result has been to make these quarries very valuable pieces of property, and to put very handsome profits into the pockets of their owners; profits which represent practically so much money which Congress has ordered those who use ornamental marble to pay over to the quarry-owners.[1]

Wool and woollens, copper, steel rails, marble, which we have now considered, are sufficient examples of the man-

[1] In regard to the duty on marble, see " Tariff Commission Report," pp. 227, 1560, 1648.

ner in which duties, already raised to high figures during the war, were still further increased after the war, for the benefit of the domestic producers. Other instances could be given in which an equal disregard Other of the consumer and taxpayer has been examples, shown. The duty on flax, the raw material flax, nickel. of a manufacture not over-prosperous, had been $15 per ton in 1864; in 1870 it was raised to $20 on undressed flax, and to $40 on dressed flax. Nickel had been admitted free of duty in 1861, and had paid only fifteen per cent. by the act of 1864. In 1870 the duty was sudenly made thirty cents per pound, or about forty per cent. on the value. Nickel, like marble, is produced in only one locality in this country. There exists a single nickel mine, in Pennsylvania, owned by a well-known advocate of protection, and, with the aid of the tariff, this mine, doubtless, has yielded the owner very handsome returns.[1] Examples need not be multiplied. Enough has

---

[1] Mr. Joseph Wharton, of Philadelphia, is the owner of the nickel mine. Mr. Wharton has also been largely interested in Bessemer steel-works. There can be no impropriety in mentioning his name, as he has publicly advocated not only the general doctrine of protection, but also the retention of the duties on nickel and steel. See "Tariff Com. Report," pp. 201–204; and *ibid.*, 219, 393, in regard to the effect of the duty on nickel. *Cf.* Mr. Wharton's pamphlet, "The Duty on Nickel," Philadelphia, 1883; and Mr. D. A. Wells's remarks on this pamphlet in *Princeton Review*, July, 1883, pp. 8–11. See also "Mineral Resources of the United States," p. 405. Mr. Wharton is the founder of the Wharton School of Finance and Economy, in Philadelphia, in which protectionist doctrines are taught. Indeed, Mr. Wharton, when giving the money for founding the school, stipulated that the professors should teach "how, by suitable tariff legislation, a nation ⁴ * * may keep its productive industry alive, cheapen the cost of commodities, and

been said to show how the tendency toward high duties, which was caused by the war, continued after the war ceased, and how this tendency was taken advantage of by the home producers in order to obtain a degree of protection which, under ordinary circumstances, they would not have dreamed of asking.

No excuse can be found for the great increase of duties on wool and woollens, on copper, and on the other articles which have been dealt with in the present chapter. That duties were greatly increased during the course of the war, and in many cases increased wantonly and unnecessarily, may be explained and in some degree excused by the imperative need of heavy taxation at that time, and by the impossibility of avoiding mistakes and incongruities in the hurried passage of a complicated mass of legislation. The retention of these war taxes, heavy and often exorbitant as they were, for twenty years after the occasion for them had passed, is not indeed to be defended, but it may be reasonably explained. The pressure of other problems, the fear of infringing on vested rights and interests, the powerful opposition which is always met in withdrawing public bounty when once it has been conferred, may explain the failure to reduce the war duties on grounds which, if not sufficient, are at least not unbecoming to our public life. But for the additions

Character of these measures.

---

oblige foreigners to sell it at low prices, while contributing largely toward defraying the expense of its government." The quotation is from the letter of gift.

to the protective system that were made by measures like the woollens act of 1867 and the copper act of 1869, no explanation can be given that does not reflect in some degree on the good name and the good faith of the national legislature. Such measures can be accounted for only when we call to mind that our public life was demoralized during the years immediately following the war; that jobs were plenty and lobbyists powerful; that some Congressmen thought it not improper to favor legislation that put money into their own pockets, and many thought it quite proper to support legislation that put money into the pockets of influential constituents. The measures which we have been considering were by no means the most conspicuous or the worst results of this state of things. Bribery, direct or indirect, is not likely to have been used to affect tariff provisions; it certainly can have had little influence on legislation. Contributions to the party chest are the form in which money payments by the protected interests are likely to have been made, so far as such payments were made at all. But the general laxity of thought on public trusts undoubtedly made possible the manipulation of the tariff in the interest of private individuals. The tone of political life, as indeed that of commercial life, was lowered by the abnormal economic conditions that followed the war; and the general demoralization enabled the protected interests and their champions to rush through Congress measures which, in a more healthy state of public affairs, would have been reprobated and rejected.

CHAPTER IV.

THE TARIFF ACT OF 1883.

In the preceding chapters the tariff has been discussed independently of the act of 1883. That act, aside from the abortive horizontal reduction of 1872, made the first general revision since the Civil War. It has been assumed, in our discussion of the legislation previous to 1883, that the revision was not so complete, and the change made in the course of it not sufficiently great, to affect the substantial truth of the statement that the war duties are still retained as the basis of our tariff system. It remains to justify this assumption by examining in some detail the act of 1883.

The history of the passage of the act is so recent and familiar that only the salient events need be recalled. After the crisis of 1873 little or nothing was heard for a while about the tariff; and so habituated had the public become to the extreme protective régime that the demand for its reform met with little support. The subject was again made prominent, after having attracted little attention for several years, by the redundant revenue which was the consequence of the revival of trade in 1879 and the subsequent years. The connection between tariff legislation and the state of the revenue has indeed been curiously constant in our history. In 1842 an empty treasury was followed by the passage of a high protective tariff. In 1857 an overflowing revenue caused a reduction of the duties. In 1861 the Morrill tariff was passed, partly in order to make good a deficit. During the war the need of money alone made possible the act of 1864. The ten per cent. reduction of 1872 was called out Agitation largely by the redundant revenue; its abolition on the tariff in 1875 was excused by the falling off in the 'renewed. government income. In recent years the surplus has been on the average about a hundred millions a year,[1] and the demand for a reduction in the tariff rates has become steadily stronger.

In 1882 a protectionist Congress passed an act for the appointment of a Tariff Commission, Tariff which was to report at the next session of Commission Congress what changes it thought desirable. of 1882. Of the gentlemen appointed by the President on this commission a majority were advocates of high protection; while no member could be said to represent that part of the public which believed a reduction of the protective duties to be desirable. Mr. John L. Hayes,

---

[1] The surplus, after paying all expenses and interest on the public debt, was:

In the fiscal year	1880	.	.	.	.	.	$65,883,000
"	"	1881	.	.	.	.	.	100,069,000
"	"	1882	.	.	.	.	.	145,543,000
"	"	1883	.	.	.	.	.	132,879,000
"	"	1884	.	.	.	.	.	104,393,000,

(under the act of 1883).

the secretary of the Wool Manufacturers' Association, was president of the commission. Its report was laid before Congress at the beginning of the session of 1882-83. At first no action on this report or on the tariff seemed likely to be taken ; for the House, in which revenue bills must originate, was unable to agree on any bill. But the House, having passed a bill for the reduction of some of the internal taxes, the Senate tacked to this bill, as an amendment, a tariff bill based, in the main, on the recommendations of the Tariff Commission. When this bill came before the House the protectionists again succeeded, as in 1872, in obtaining a parliamentary victory. By an adroit manœuvre they managed to have it referred to a conference committee.[1]   In this committee the details of the tariff act were finally settled ; for the bill, as reported

---

[1] This manœuvre was a curious example of the manner in which the rules of Congress are manipulated in order to affect legislation. A two-thirds vote, by the existing rules, was required to bring the Senate bill before the House.   A two-thirds majority in favor of the bill could not be obtained ; though it was probable that on a direct vote a majority in its favor could have been got.   The protectionists wished to have the bill referred to a conference committee, which would probably act in the direction desired by them. For this purpose a resolution was introduced by Mr. Reed, of Maine, providing for a *new rule* of the House, by which a bare majority was to have power to take up a bill amended by the Senate for the purpose of non-concurrence in the Senate amendments, *but not for the purpose of concurrence.* By the passage of this rule a majority of the House could take up the tariff bill, and then *refuse* to concur in the Senate amendments ; but under this rule the amendments could not be concurred in.   There was, consequently, no possibility of passing the tariff bill in the shape in which it came from the Senate.   The bill had to be referred to a conference committee ; and in that committee, as the text states, the details of the bill were settled.   The Reed rule, though made a permanent rule of the House, was passed merely in order to attain this object.

to the Senate and House by the conferees of the two bodies, was passed by them and became law. Act of 1883: The object of the manœuvre was to check the how passed. reduction of duties as it appeared in the Senate bill; and this object was attained. The changes made by the conference committees were, as a rule, in a protectionist direction. The duties on a number of articles were raised by the committee above the rates of the Senate bill, and even above the rates which the House had shown a willingness to accept. The consequence was that the tariff act, as finally passed, contained a much less degree of reduction than the original Senate bill; and it was passed in the Senate only by a strict party vote of 32 to 31, while the original Senate bill had been passed by a vote of 42 to 19.[1]

---

[1] Mr. Morrison said, in the last session of Congress (1883–84), in commenting on the act of 1883 · " The office and duty of a conference committee is to adjust the difference between two disagreeing Houses. This House had decided that bar-iron of the middle class should pay $20 a ton; the Senate that it was to pay $20.16 a ton. The gentlemen of the conference committee reconciled this difference—how? By raising bar-iron [of this class] above both House and Senate to $22.40 a ton. The Tariff Commission reported that the ·tariff on iron ore should be 50 cents a ton. The Senate said it should be 50 cents a ton. The House said it should be 50 cents a ton. Gentlemen of the conference committee reconciled the agreement of the House, Senate, and Tariff Commission into a disagreement, and made the duty on iron ore 75 cents a ton. The gentlemen of the conference did a similar service for the great corporation of corporations, the Iron and Steel Association, by giving it a tax of $17 on steel rails, which the House had fixed at $15 and the Senate at $15.68 per ton." Quoted in Nelson's " Unjust Tariff Law," pp. 22, 23. *Cf.* remarks to the same effect by Senator Beck, who was a member of the conference committee.—*Cong. Record*, 1883–84, p. 2786.

The conferees for the Senate were Messrs. Morrill, Sherman, Aldrich,

In taking up the provisions of the act of 1883,[1] it will be best to consider first those cases in which an increase in the duties has been made. For, unexpected as it may be to the reader of the preceding pages, the act of 1883 contains a number of sections in which protective duties have been advanced above

Duties raised in 1883.

the rates of preceding acts; and these sections are very instructive when we try to make out the general character of the new act. To begin with, the duties on certain classes of woollen goods have been raised. On most woollens the figures have been lowered; though, as will be seen, the reduction in these cases has not been such as to bring any benefit to consumers. But on certain classes of woollens, on which a reduction of duty, if made, would have been of benefit to consumers, the duties have not been reduced, but advanced. This is the case

Woollen dress goods.

with dress goods made wholly of wool. Under the act of 1867 such goods had paid a maximum duty of eight cents per yard and forty per cent. It will be observed that the forty per cent. rate on these goods had already been above the general *ad-valorem* duty

---

Bayard, and Beck ; for the House, Messrs. Kelley, McKinley, Haskell, Randall, and Carlisle. All but three (Bayard, Beck, and Carlisle) were strong protectionists.

[1] In the appendix, VII., the reader will find a table giving in detail the old duties, those recommended by the Tariff Commission, and those now in force, on all articles mentioned in this chapter. In the document entitled " Tariff Compilation," printed by the Senate in 1884, a complete list of the old and new duties is given.

of thirty-five per cent. established by the act of 1867. Nevertheless the act of 1883 increased the duty on these goods to nine cents a yard and forty per cent. The Tariff Commission had even recommended twelve cents a yard and forty per cent. Goods of this class form the largest single item in the importations of woollens into the United States. They are made to no very great extent by the domestic manufacturers. The new duty is intended to enable the latter to engage profitably in making them ; since the old duty, though it amounted in all to more than sixty-five per cent. on the values of the imports, had not sufficed for this purpose. No pretence was made that this increase in the specific duty was necessary to give more effective compensation for the wool duty ; in fact, as we shall see, the duty on wool was slightly lowered, so that the compensating duty, if changed at all, should have gone down. The new duty was simply a concession to the demand of the manufacturers for still further protection on one of the few articles on which the previous rates had still permitted foreign competition.[1]

Next to dress goods, such as were discussed in the preceding paragraph, the class of woollens of which

---

[1] The Tariff Commission, in its " Report " (p. 31), says : " The new clause in relation to all-wool merino goods is a new provision, and has in view the introduction of fabrics never yet successfully made in this country. Many of these goods constitute staple fabrics * * * and their manufacture would be a desirable acquisition to our national industry." *Cf.*, on the whole of the new system of wool and woollen duties, two articles in *Bulletin Wool Mf.*, xiii., 1-13, 89-128.

the importations are largest are the finer grades of cloths and cassimeres. The importation of these goes on

Woollen cloths. steadily in large quantities, and the tariff tax on them is felt with its full weight; for, since importation continues, it is clear, that not only the imported goods, but also those of the same kind made at home, are raised in price to the full extent of the duty. The duty on them, like that on dress goods, is one of the comparatively few in the woollens schedule which has not been entirely prohibitory. The production of these finer woollens is carried on in this country only to a limited extent. It is not surprising, therefore, to find here also a rise of the rates in the new act. Cloths are there divided into two classes: those costing more and those costing less than eighty cents per pound. The latter, costing less than eighty cents, are admitted, as before, at an *ad-valorem* duty of thirty-five per cent. But the former, costing more than eighty cents, per pound, are now made to pay forty per cent. The specific compensating duty is indeed reduced somewhat in both cases, in connection with the lower duties on wool, which will presently be discussed; but the *ad-valorem* rate, that which is avowedly protective, is increased.

A change of almost the same kind was made in the

Cotton goods. duties on cotton goods. Here also the duty was lowered on the common grades of goods; and on these grades, as will be seen in the following, the reduction was again a purely nominal one, of no benefit to the consumers and taxpayers. But on other grades of cotton goods, whose importation still goes on, and on which a decrease in the duty would have caused some lowering of prices and some relief from taxation, there was no reduction, but an increase. The duty on cotton hosiery, embroideries, trimming, laces, insertings, etc., had been thirty-five per cent. under the old law. In the act of 1883 it was made to be forty per cent. The duty of thirty-five per cent. had been imposed during the war, in 1864, at a time when raw cotton was taxed, and the manufactured cotton also paid a heavy internal tax. This rate remained unchanged from 1864 till 1883, notwithstanding the abolition of the internal taxes; and now it has even been raised to forty per cent. The importance of this change is clear only when we know that imports of cottons consist chiefly of goods of the class on which the duty is increased. The statistics of former years are so arranged that we cannot tell exactly how large a proportion these goods bear to the total imports of cottons; but it is safe to say that more than half the cotton goods which continue to be brought into this country from abroad will be affected by the increase of duty from thirty-five to forty per cent.[1]

The process by which the protective system has gradu-

---

[1] The goods on which the new duty took effect are separately stated for the first time in the statistical returns for 1883-84. From the statement of imports for the ten months ending April, 1884 (the only statement the writer has at hand), it appears that out of a total importation of about $25,000,000 of cottons, not less than $15,000,000 paid the new duty of forty per cent.

ally been brought to include almost every article, whatever its character, whose production in the
country is possible, is illustrated by the new
duty on iron ore. This, as the crudest of raw materials, would be admitted free, or at very low rates,
according to ordinary canons of protection. In 1861 it
had paid a duty of ten per cent. as an unenumerated
article ; and this rate had not been changed during
the war, since the article was not one likely to be imported or to yield revenue. In 1870, when the protective principle, as we have seen, was applied with greater
strictness in various directions, the duty was raised to
twenty per cent. In recent years iron ore has been imported in considerable quantities from Spain ; and now the
duty has been raised, in the present tariff, to seventy-five
cents per ton, or about thirty-five per cent. on the value.

Iron ore.

Still another instance of the advance of duties in the
existing act is to be found in the rates on certain manufactures of steel. Here, as has so often happened,
the increase is concealed under what is in appearance merely a change in classification. The duties on
steel ingots, bars, sheets, and coils had been, until 1883,
those fixed in the war tariff of 1864,—from two and one
quarter cents to three and one half cents per pound, varying
with the value of the steel. The act of 1883 apparently
reduced these duties slightly, making them from two to
three and a quarter cents per pound. But previous to 1883
" steel, in forms not otherwise specified," had been admitted

Steel.

at a duty of thirty per cent. Under this provision, which had been in force since 1864, a number of articles, like cogged ingots, rods, piston-rods, steamer shafts, and so on, had paid only thirty per cent. The act of 1883, however, specifically enumerated these and other articles, and put them in the same schedule with steel ingots and bars,— that is, compelled them to pay a duty of from two to three and a quarter cents a pound. In almost all cases these articles now must pay three and a quarter cents a pound, which will be a considerable advance over the previous rate of thirty per cent. On the newly-enumerated articles the present act causes an increase in the duty; although, at first sight, the new schedule of steel ingots, bars, etc., seems to show a lowering of the rate.

In very much the same way, by means of a change in classification, an increase has been brought about in the duty on files. These had paid, before 1883, a duty varying, according to the length of the files, from six to ten cents *per pound*, and, in addition, thirty per cent. The Tariff Commission recommended, and the act of 1883 established, a new rate of from thirty-five cents to $2.50 *per dozen*. The effect of the change was to increase the duty on the small sizes of files. These sizes alone will feel any effect from the new duty. Under the old duty the importation of most classes of files had entirely ceased; but small files, such as are used chiefly by watchmakers, continued to be imported from Switzerland and England. On these the new classification brought about an increase

Files.

in the duty, which, it is needless to say, operated greatly to the advantage of the domestic manufacturers of the article.

Again, quicksilver had been admitted in previous years *Other articles.* free of duty; the act of 1883, in response to a demand from the owners of the richest mines in the world, those of California, imposed on this metal a duty of ten per cent.[1] One of the important drag-net paragraphs in the tariff—" manufactures, articles, vessels, and wares, not otherwise provided for, of brass, iron, lead, pewter, and tins "—shows an increase in the duty from thirty-five to forty-five per cent. A very large number of articles, tools, and machinery of various kinds are charged with duty under this clause: the imports of manufacturers of iron alone, on which the higher rate of forty-five per cent. will take effect, amounted in 1883 to nearly \$3,400,000. Other instances of the same kind could be found in the new act; but enough have been given to show that the process of extending and increasing the protective duties, which was traced in part in the preceding chapter, by no means ceased in the act of 1883.

The reader may be weary of the dry figures of the preceding paragraphs, and especially of those relating to articles of little importance, like watchmakers' files. It is true that the economic welfare of the country is not perceptibly affected by an increase in the duty on watch-

---

[1] See " Tariff Commission Report," pp. 2591–2597.

makers' files and by the consequent rise in their price. But the tariff contains a mass of these duties, which, taken together, have no small influence on the prosperity of the country; and it is im- possible to understand the history of the tariff

This increase of duties not defensi- ble.

or its effects without going more or less into details of this kind. Moreover, in regard to this act of 1883, the many instances in which duties have been advanced deserve especial attention, because they throw light on the character of the act and the intentions of those who passed it. That these changes are not defensible on any sound economic principles need not here be shown. They are to be condemned when we look at them from the point of view not only of economic principle, but of public policy and public faith. The Tariff Commission was given the task of revising the tariff "judiciously"; its recommendations were declared to contain a general reduction of duties by twenty per cent. or more, and the declared object of the leaders of the dominant party was to bring about some substantial relief. No one can doubt that "reform" at the present time means a reduction, and excludes an increase in duties, and that the advance in the rates on cottons, woollens, and other articles was no part of what the public reasonably expected in the new act. Whatever may be the feeling as to the retention of the existing duties, or as to the time and manner in which reduction should be made, public opinion with the majority of the people may be safely said to be opposed to any further growth of the protective system. No rational and unprejudiced person will deny that protection has at least been carried far enough in our tariff system. Had the higher duties of the act of 1883 been brought before Congress in a separate bill, there can be no doubt that their enactment would have been impossible. That they were in many cases half concealed by means of changes in classification, or were coupled with apparent reductions on other articles in the same schedules, shows that the protectionists themselves had some fear of putting them nakedly before the public. The existence of changes of this kind causes a feeling of suspicion as to the new tariff act as a whole. It makes a doubt arise whether in those cases where the figures have been lowered, any thing has really been done that gives relief from the burden of the protective duties.

The schedules in the tariff which have the greatest effect on the welfare of the country are those fixing the duties on iron and wool; and to these we will first give our attention. The change in the duty on wool was sufficiently simple. The *ad-valorem* rate was taken off. The duty of 1867, it will be remembered, had been, on wools costing less than thirty-two cents, ten cents per pound and eleven per cent. *ad valorem*, and, on wools costing more than thirty-two cents, twelve cents per pound plus ten per cent. *ad valorem*. These *ad-valorem* rates of eleven and

Reductions of duty: wool.

ten per cent. were taken off, and the rates left simply at ten and twelve cents per pound.[1] In regard to the greater part of the wools raised in the United States, this reduction is purely nominal. It leaves the duty on the cheaper grades of wool raised in Texas and in the Territories at a point where it is still entirely prohibitory. That such is the case, has been frankly acknowledged in the official mouth-piece of the wool manufacturers.[2] So far as concerns the higher grades of wool, such as are raised in Ohio and neighboring States, the reduction is a slight substantial gain. The only objection is that it does not go far enough. The duty on wool, notwithstanding the cumbrous machinery of compensating duties, undoubtedly has a hampering influence on the wool manufacture, and has been an important factor in confining this industry within a limited range that is often complained of. Like

---

[1] The duty in the act of 1883 is ten cents on wool costing *thirty* cents or less, and twelve cents on that costing more than thirty cents. The change (in the line of division, according to value) from thirty-two to thirty cents is not without importance ; and, as far as it goes, it evidently tends to neutralize the reduction. This is confessed in the *Bulletin Wool Mf.*, xiii., 11, 109.

The duty on carpet wool (*ante* p. 47) was also reduced from three and six cents per pound to two and one half and five cents. There is no reason why carpet wool should not have been admitted entirely free of duty, since such wool is hardly raised in this country at all. (See " Tariff Comm. Report," pp. 2335–2338.) The retention of the duty on it is doubtless explained by the fact that the compensating specific duty on carpets, like most of the compensating duties, in reality yields a good deal of protection to the manufacturers ; this they are unwilling to give up ; and they cannot retain it without also retaining the duty on carpet wool, that being the only foundation for the specific compensating duty.

[2] See *Bulletin Wool Mf.*, xiii., 100.

every protective duty, it causes consumers to pay a tax which does not go into the government coffers, but merely aids or enriches individuals. As a tax on raw materials, it tends to bear with heavier weight than would be the case with the same duty on a finished product ; since it is advanced again and again by the wool dealer, the manufacturer, the cloth dealers, the tailor, each of whom must have a greater profit in proportion to the greater amount of capital which the wool duty and the higher price of wool make it necessary for him to employ. So strong and so clear are the objections to duties of this kind that hardly another civilized country, whatever its general policy, attempts to protect wool.[1] Moreover, the reduction of a duty of this kind can take place with exceptional ease. Wool is not produced, as a rule, in large quantities, by persons who devote themselves exclusively to this as a business. It is mainly produced by farmers, whose chief income comes from other sources, and on whom a reduction of duty and a fall of price would fall with comparatively little weight.[2] The case is different in many branches of manufacture, where a considerable

---

[1] Not only England, but Germany, France, Austria, and Italy, all of whom maintain a more or less protective tariff, and grow large quantities of wool, admit this material free of duty.

[2] It may be said that this is not the case with the large sheep ranches of the Western States and Territories. But these ranches, it happens, produce the grades of wool of which the price is least affected by the duty ; and moreover, the production of these wools has been exceptionally profitable (partly in consequence of the tariff), and such fall in price as would ensue could very well be endured by the producers. See " Tariff Comm. Report," pp. 1782–1785, and the passages in *Bulletin Wool Mf.* already referred to.

fall in prices may produce an entire cessation of production and a great disturbance of economic relations, and
where in consequence a reduction of protection must be
made more gradually and carefully. The wool duty may
be reduced quickly and sharply without any great danger
of interfering harmfully with the established state of
things. All economic experience, and more especially
the lessons of the last few years, show that such a change
is likely to come in the near future.

We turn now to the reductions of duty in the new act
on woollen goods, which must follow from the
lower duty on wool. It has been seen that
Woollens.
the *ad-valorem*, or protective, duty was not decreased
at all, and that on the finer classes of woollens it was
increased from thirty-five to forty per cent. But the
specific, or compensating, duty was reduced from fifty
cents to thirty-five cents a pound. The present duty is
thirty-five cents a pound and thirty-five per cent. on
woollens costing less than eighty cents per pound, and
thirty-five cents and forty per cent. on woollens costing
more than eighty cents. The lowering of the specific
duty was in part called for by the reduction of the duty
on wool; but the decrease is somewhat larger than the
reduced duty on the raw material made necessary. The
compensating duty in the new act seems to be fixed on
the assumption that no more than three and one half
pounds of wool are used in making a pound of cloth;
whereas the act of 1867, it will be remembered, was

framed on the basis of four pounds of wool to the pound of cloth. This may be called a tacit confession that the compensating duty of 1867 was excessive ; and the new arrangement takes away some of the protection which was formerly given by the specific duty. But this change is of little, if any, benefit to consumers. So far as the finer grades of woollens are concerned, it is more than offset by the increase in the *ad-valorem* duty from thirty-five to forty per cent. So far as the cheaper grades of woollens are concerned, it has no real effect. The duty on these was prohibitory before, and it remains prohibitory now. A reduction of a prohibitory duty may be made and still leave the rate so high as to shut out importation; and this is what has been done. Such a change has no effect on trade or prices, and brings no benefit to consumers. Precisely similar is the state of things in regard to flannels, blankets, and similar goods. On these also the specific duty has been reduced,—on the cheapest grades from a rate of twenty cents a pound to rates of ten and twelve cents. But the new rates are still high enough to shut out importation, and bring about no change beyond that of the figures on the statute-book.[1]

---

[1] The manufacturers assert that the duties on goods have been reduced more in proportion than those on wool. See Mr. Hayes's article in *Bulletin Wool Mf.*, vol. xiii. Complaints are particularly strong from the manufacturers of yarns, who say that the readjustment of duties on the new tariff enables yarns to be imported from England too easily ; and it seems there is ground for this complaint, to the extent that on some yarns the duty, in comparison with the duty on the wool, is too low.—See *Bureau of Statistics Report* for quarter ending June, 1884, pp. 564–566.

Changes of precisely this kind are to be found in other parts of the new act. The rates on the cheap grades of cotton goods, for instance, show a considerable reduction. On the lowest class

Cottons.

of unprinted goods the duty had been five cents per yard; it is two and one half cents by the new act. But the old duty has for many years ceased to have any appreciable effect on the prices of cotton goods. The common grades of cottons can be made, as a rule, as cheaply in this country as anywhere in the world; in fact, some of them are regularly exported in large quantities.[1] If the duty on such cottons were entirely abolished, it is probable that they could not be imported; and it is certain that a very small duty would suffice to shut out from our market all foreign competitors in them. Under these circumstances the lowering of the rate of duty which the new act makes, is of no effect whatever. The same holds good of almost all the various reductions in the specific duties on plain and printed cotton goods. These changes are in no sense a reduction of taxation. On the other hand, in the case of the finer cotton goods, laces, trimmings, etc., on which a lowering of the rates would have brought about a real relief from taxation, there was, as we have seen, no decrease, but an increase in the new act.

The duty on pig-iron was reduced by the new act from

---

[1] See the remarks of the report on the Cotton Manufacture, in the volume of the Census of 1880 on Manufactures.

$7.00 to $6.72 a ton.   This change is insignificant, hardly
two per cent. on the foreign price of iron.   A
greater could have been made without danger of
any disturbance of the iron trade.   So far as it goes, it is in
the right direction.   The same general remark is to be made
of the reduction on bar-iron, which, on the ordinary grade,
lowers the duty from one cent a pound to eight tenths
of a cent.   The reduction on bar-iron is, indeed, a change of
the same kind as the reduction on cottons, on woollens,
and on many other articles,—it still leaves the duty still
high enough to prevent any lowering of prices and any
effect on trade.[1]   The duties on the various forms of
manufactured iron—hoop, band, sheet, plate iron, etc.—
have gone down in much the same way.   The reductions
were slight in all cases, and often merely nominal.   It is
safe to say that, in general, the new rates on iron and its
manufactures can have no appreciable effect on the trade
and welfare of the country.

Iron.

The duty on steel rails shows a considerable
reduction.   The old rate was $28.00 a ton, and
the rate now in force is $17.00.   If this change had been
made four or five years ago, it would have been of much

Steel rails.

---

[1] A manufacturer of iron, operating near the sea-shore, admitted that in
October, 1882,—not a time of special depression,—the price of domestic
bar-iron was lower by $5.00 than the price for which foreign iron could be
imported ; and that the price in Pittsburg was lower by $10.00 than iron could
be imported for.   The change in duty under the act was one fifth of a cent
per pound, or $4.48 per gross ton : that is, less than the reduction of $5.00,
which it was admitted that the manufacturers on the sea-shore (not to mention those of Pittsburg) could "stand." "Tariff Comm. Report," pp.
2458, 2459.

practical importance ; but for the immediate present and possibly in the future, it has no effect whatever. It has already been said that, after the enormous profits made by the steel-rail makers in 1879–1881, the production in this country was greatly increased. At the same time the demand from the railroads fell off ; and the huge quantities which the mills were able to turn out could be disposed of, if at all, only at prices greatly reduced. The consequence is that the price of rails, which in 1880 was higher than the English price by the full extent of the duty of $28.00, is now comparatively little above it.[1] The price here is still above the English rate ; but the difference is less than $17.00 a ton ; and the duty of that amount is still sufficient to keep out foreign rails. The reduction of the duty has therefore had no effect on prices, and has brought no immediate benefit to consumers ; and for the present, like the changes already noticed in regard to cottons and woollens, it is merely a lowering of the figures on the statute-book. Possibly in the future, when railroad building is again pushed, and the demand for rails quickens, it may have some effect. It will then prevent the rail-makers from pushing their prices quite up to the extravagant figures of past years. The probability is, to be sure, that this could not be done even if the old duty had been retained, since the knowledge of the process and the facilities for production have been so greatly extended within the last

[1] See appendix, VI.

two or three years.   But the change in the duty at least
reduces one factor of those that made the great steel-rail
"boom" of 1880 a possibility.

Analogous in its effects to the reduction on steel rails,
is that on copper.   The duty on this article goes
Copper.   down from five cents, the rate imposed in 1869,
to four cents a pound.   It has been shown in the preceding pages that the duty on copper enured almost exclusively to the benefit of the owners of the copper mines of
Lake Superior, who were enabled by it to combine and fix
the price of copper without fear of competition from abroad.
The great profits of their mines caused them steadily to increase their product; and although much of their surplus
has been disposed of abroad, at prices lower than those
demanded at home, the growing supply caused the
domestic price slowly to fall.   The discovery of large
deposits of copper, in recent years, in Montana and Ari-
zona, and the shipment to market of a great deal of copper
from these sources, have at the same time broken the
monopoly of the Lake Superior combination, and caused
the price to go down still further.   Importation of copper
in any considerable quantities ceased many years ago; and
in face of the recent fall in the domestic price, imports
would not be resumed even if a somewhat greater reduction of duty were made than is contained in the new tariff.
In the last two or three years, the domestic competition has
been so strong that the price in this country has been,
quality for quality, hardly three cents above the price

abroad.' Under such conditions a reduction of the duty from five to four cents a pound evidently has no immediate effect. It is true that the duty of four cents a pound still makes it possible that in the future a combination of the copper producers may again raise their prices at the expense of consumers. Such a result, it is said, is far from impossible, since the product of the Western mines is unsteady, and not unlikely to cease altogether; which would leave the field free once more to the Lake Superior producers. A complete abolition of the duty on copper could be made now without causing any appreciable disturbance of trade, and it would prevent for the future a repetition of the abuses of the past.

The duty on marble in the new act is fixed at sixty-five cents per cubic foot on rough marble, and at $1.10 per cubic foot on marble sawed, dress- Other reductions. ed, and in slabs. This is hardly a perceptible decrease from the compound duties which were discussed in the preceding chapter.' The duty on nickel was put at fifteen cents a pound, in place of the previous duty of twenty and thirty cents a pound. Practically all the nickel imported in recent years has come in at a duty of twenty cents; consequently the reduction is less than it seems to be on the surface.' It is worth while to note that in both these cases the Tariff Commission

---

[1] See appendix V., for complete tables of the prices, imports, and exports of copper.

[2] See *ante*, p. 70.

[3] See " Tariff Comm. Report," pp. 201, 202.

had recommended rates that would practically have increased the duty. In both, a sharper reduction would have caused no disturbance of trade or of production. Not a few changes were made which can be commended, in the same way, without any qualification except that they were exceedingly moderate. A fair example of these is the reduction of the duty on manufactures of silk from sixty to fifty per cent. In practice the old duty had been equivalent to not more than fifty per cent. on the actual value of the goods, because of the regular and steady undervaluation of silk imports. Such undervaluations, and the concomitant practice of false invoicing, are the inevitable result of high *ad-valorem* duties; and they will probably continue to exist under the new duty of fifty per cent., and will make that again equivalent in fact to forty or forty-five per cent. The silk manufacturers of this country attempted to contrive a schedule of specific duties on silks; but their scheme was not satisfactory, as indeed might have been expected from the greatly varying character of the goods. The *ad-valorem* method was retained, with the reduced rate. The reduction is as great as could have been expected under the circumstances, and possibly as great as was wise at so short notice. The duty must be still considered much too high, whether we look at it from the economic, or from the fiscal and administrative point of view.[1] The change in the duty on silks is perhaps the greatest effective reduction in the new

---

[1] On the silk duties, see "Tariff Comm. Report," pp. 2165–2174.

tariff act. Others of the same kind are the lowering of the rate on finer linens, from forty to thirty-five per cent.; the decrease of the specific duty on cotton bagging; and so on with a considerable number of articles.

It is interesting to note that the duties on a number of agricultural or mainly agricultural pro- Wheat, ducts, such as beef and pork, hams and corn, etc. bacon, lard, cheese, butter, wheat, corn, and oats, are left unchanged in the act of 1883. The duty on barley was somewhat lowered, at the request of the brewers of beer; and that on rice also was slightly reduced. But almost all of these products continue to be charged with the same rates as in previous years. It is needless to say that the duties on them have no effect whatever, except to an insignificant extent on the local trade across the Canadian border. Articles such as these, which are steadily exported, are not affected by import duties. The duties probably are left unchanged in order to maintain the fiction that the agricultural population gets through them a share of the benefits of protection. It is curious that the reductions in this schedule, on barley and on rice, affect almost the only products on which the duties in fact bring any benefit to the agricultural producer and any burden for the consumer.

Enough has been said of the details of General the changes made by the act of 1883. Its remarks. general character cannot easily be described. In truth, it can hardly be said to have any general character.

It is best described as a half-hearted and unsuccessful attempt on the part of protectionists to bring about an apparent reform of the tariff.[1] That it was framed by men who at heart were protectionists, and who had no conviction that protection in this country had been carried too far, or even far enough, is shown by the numerous cases in which, more or less openly, an increase in protective taxes was made. On the other hand, the desire to make some concession to the growing popular feeling against excessive duties caused reductions to be made—sometimes reductions that gave a real, though slight, relief from the burden of the duties, but more often reductions such as had little effect other than the change of the figures on the statute-book. On the whole, the changes have clearly not been of enough importance to affect the essential character of our tariff system. That system still retains, substantially unchanged, those high duties which were imposed during the war, and those further protective duties which the weakness of Congress, the general disorder of public affairs, and the insistence of domestic producers, brought about in the years immediately following the war. It is

---

[1] Mr. John L. Hayes, the President of the Tariff Commission, writing more particularly of the new duties on wool and woollens, said, shortly after the passage of the act : " Reduction in itself was by no means desirable to us ; it was a concession to public sentiment, a bending of the top and branches to the wind of public opinion to save the trunk of the protective system. In a word, the object was *protection through reduction.* We were willing to concede only to save the essentials both of the wool and woollens tariff. * * * We wanted the tariff to be made by our friends."—*Bulletin Wool Mf.*, xiii., 94.

still a system which, if proposed in time of peace as a substitute for the duties in force in 1860, would be rejected as excessive and unreasonable.

Since the passage of the act of 1883, several unsuccessful attempts have been made to amend it.[1] In 1884, Mr. Morrison, of Illinois, introduced a bill by which a general reduction of twenty per cent., and the entire remission of duties on iron ore, coal, lumber, and other articles, were proposed.   Mr. Morrison may have been moved to advocate the plan of a "horizontal" reduction by the example which the Republicans had set in 1872; and doubtless he was also influenced by the circumstance that the protectionists themselves had arranged the details of the act of 1883, and could not complain of disproportionate reductions, or of a disturbance of relative rates, under a plan which affected all articles equally.   Nevertheless, the proposal met with vehement opposition not only from the Republicans, but from a strong minority in Mr. Morrison's own party.   It was disposed of on May 6, 1884, by a vote (156 to 151) striking out its enacting clause. Two years later, in the Forty-ninth Congress, a similar disposition was made of another bill introduced by Morrison.   The proposal of 1886, however, was different from that of 1884, in that it made detailed changes in the duties.   Lumber, salt, wool, hemp, flax, and other articles were put on the free list; the duty on woollens was made

---

[1] An excellent account of these attempts is given by Mr. O. H. Perry in the *Quarterly Journal of Economics* for October, 1887, vol. II., pp. 69–79.

35 per cent., the specific duties on woollens being removed with the duties on wool; and reductions were proposed on cottons and on sugar. The bill never was discussed in Congress, for Mr. Morrison's motion to proceed
to its consideration was defeated by a vote of 157 to 140,
and during the rest of the session no further attempt was
made to take it up. Early in the next session, in December, 1886, a motion was again made to proceed to the
consideration of revenue bills, and again was defeated.
Some other measures of less significance were also introduced in these years, such as a bill of 1884, to restore the
duties of 1867 on wool, which was defeated by a close
vote of 126 to 119, and bills introduced by Messrs. Randall and Hiscock in 1886. Mr. Randall's bill proposed
the removal of internal taxes on tobacco, fruit brandies,
and spirits used in the arts, entire remission of duties on
lumber, jute butts, and a few minor articles, and a slight
reduction of some other duties. Mr. Hiscock's bill proposed similar changes in the internal taxes, and a large
reduction of the duty on sugar, with a bounty to American sugar-makers. Both of these bills, which indicate the
manner in which the protectionists tried to grapple with
the problem of reducing the revenue, were referred to the
Committee of Ways and Means, and, not being reported
from that body, never came to a vote in the House.

It may be an indication of some change in public
opinion that the minority among the Democratic Congressmen, by whom the consideration of tariff bills has

been opposed, has become less strong in the last few years. The Democrats have had the control of the House since 1884, but have been divided on the tariff question. In 1884, 41 Democrats voted against Mr. Morrison's horizontal bill, while 151 voted for it; in June, 1886, 35 Democrats voted against the tariff bill of that year, 136 voting for it; and in December of 1886, the votes were 26 in the negative and 143 in the affirmative. The Democratic minority has steadily diminished, from 41 to 35, and between the two sessions of the Forty-ninth Congress from 35 to 26. The Republican votes on all three occasions were practically unanimous in opposition to the proposed legislation.[1]

The act of 1883 made no change that could be satisfactory to those who oppose protective duties on principle, or to that larger class whose members believe that the time has come for some modification of the existing protective system. The feeling in favor of that system, while perhaps undiminished in those parts of the country where the population is engaged very largely in protected industries, has declined perceptibly in the country at large. The redundant revenue has acted as a powerful force toward a reduction of duties, as under similar circumstances it acted in 1832–33, and again in 1857. The indications are that duties will be lowered in some moderate degree in the early future. When it is found, as beyond

---

[1] Interesting tables, by States, of these votes, will be found in Mr. Perry's article, referred to above.

doubt it will be found, that no such disastrous results
ensue as are predicted by the extreme protectionists, a
further reduction may meet with less opposition.   Certainly it is to be wished that changes from a system which
has been in force for twenty-five years, and to which the
industrial organization has more or less completely
adapted itself, may be made slowly and with caution.   It
would be a great mistake—fortunately not one likely to
be committed—if a headlong reduction like that of 1833
were again to be attempted, and were again to overshoot
the mark.   A great change in the character of our customs system, in order to be safe, must be gradual and
tentative, and is not likely to be fully carried out in less
time than has elapsed since the present system was begun.
But the permanent retention of the extreme protection
which is the unexpected residuum of the war troubles,
should not be permitted ; proposals, such as are occasionally brought forward, for the further increase of protective
duties, are to be uncompromisingly opposed ; and a careful and judicious pruning of the present duties is the
part of sound policy for the immediate future.

APPENDIX.

TABLE I.

Imports, Duties, and Ratio of Imports to Duties, 1860–1883.

(*From the* "Statistical Abstract.")

00,000 omitted.

Imports.

Fiscal Year Ending June 30.	Free.	Dutiable.	Total.	Duties Collected.	Per cent. of Duties on Dutiable Imports.	Per cent. of Duties on Aggregate Imports.
1860	73.7	279.9	353.6	52.7	19.67	15.67
1	71.1	218.2	289.3	39.0	18.84	14.21
2	52.7	136.6	189.4	46.5	36.20	26.08
3	35.2	208.1	243.3	63.7	32.62	28.28
4	41.1	275.3	316.4	96.5	36.69	32.04
5	44.5	194.2	238.7	80.6	47.56	38.46
6	59.0	375.8	434.8	177.1	48.35	41.81
7	23.1	372.6	395.7	168.5	46.67	44.56
8	15.2	342.2	357.4	160.5	48.70	46.56
9	21.6	395.9	417.5	176.6	47.36	44.76
1870	20.1	415.8	435.9	191.5	47.16	44.92
1	36.6	483.6	520.2	202.4	44.05	40.47
2	47.3	579.2	626.5	212.6	41.47	37.94
3	144.8 [1]	497.3	642.1	184.9	38.15	27.89
4	151.5	415.9	567.4	160.5	38.61	28.29
5	146.3	386.7	533.0	154.6	40.69	29.37
6	140.4	320.4	460.8	145.2	44.80	31.25
7	140.8	310.5	451.3	128.4	42.95	20.20
8	141.3	295.8	437.0	127.2	42.81	29.01
9	142.7	303.1	445.7	133.4	44.95	30.37
1880	208.3	459.6	667.9	182.7	43.56	29.12
1	202.5	440.2	642.7	193.8	43.25	29.79
2	210.6	514.1	724.6	216.1	42.70	30.18
3	207.5	515.7	723.2	210.6	42.65	30.05
4	211.3	456.3	667.6	190.3	41.70	28.5
5	192.9	386.7	579.6	178.1	46.00	30.7
6	211.5	413.8	625.3	189.4	45.80	30.0
7	233.1	450.3	683.4	188.5	47.10	27.6

[1] The abolition of the tea and coffee duties, and the free admission of some other articles, in 1872, account for the sudden increase of non-dutiable imports. See p. 186.

This table is taken from the "Statistical Abstract," and gives the computations of the Bureau of Statistics. The figures given in successive editions of the "Abstract" are not always the same, and, again, sometimes vary from those given by the Bureau in its "Reports on Commerce and Navigation." These discrepancies arise in part from varying usage. "Imports," for instance, sometimes include articles of domestic produce which have been exported and brought back, and "duties" sometimes include the internal tax then collected on such articles. Some peculiarities in the table as given above may be worth noting. The average rate on dutiable articles in 1863 is 32.62 per cent., while in 1862 the average on dutiable articles was 36.20. Yet, since duties were steadily increasing during the war, one would expect the rate to be higher in 1863 than in 1862. The explanation must be that a number of articles which before 1863 had been admitted free were subjected to rather low duties in that year, and caused a lowering of the average rate on dutiable articles; or that the importation of goods charged with high rates was exceptionally small in 1863. Both causes may have operated. It is to be remembered that, although the Morrill tariff act of 1861 went in force for the fiscal year ending June 30, 1862, the average rate of that year (36.20 on dutiable goods) does not represent the rates of the Morrill tariff. During 1861 and the early parts of 1862 several other tariff acts were passed, levying duties additional to those of the Morrill act, and going into force during that fiscal year. The effect of all these measures is seen in the average rates for the fiscal year 1861–2, which consequently do not indicate the general character of the Morrill tariff. The effect of the ten per cent. reduction of 1872 is clearly seen in the average rates of 1873 and the subsequent years.

TABLE II.

Duties on Some Important Articles, Raised during the War, and Retained without Reduction till 1883.

Articles.	Duty under the Morrill Tariff of 1861.	Duty of 1864, in Force in 1883.
Books	15 %	25 %
Chinaware, plain . .	30 %	45 %
Cotton goods, not otherwise provided for .	30 %	35 %
Cottons, coarse, unbleached . . .	1 ct. per yard.	5 cts. per yard.
Cotton spool-thread .	30 %	6 cts. per dozen, plus 30 % (= 60 to 70 %).
Cottons, fine printed .	4¼ cts. per square yard plus 10 %	5½ cts. per square yard plus 20 %
Manufactures of flax, jute, or hemp, not otherwise provided for	30 %	40 %
Glass, common window	1 to 1½ cts. per square foot.	¾ to 4 cts. per square foot.
Gloves, of kid or leather	30 %	50 %
Bar-iron [1]	⅜ ct. per ton	1 to 1½ cts. per lb.
Iron rails	$12 per ton	$14 per ton
Steel, in ingots, bars, etc.	1½ to 2 cts. per lb.	2¼ to 3½ cts. per lb.
Pig lead	1 ct. per lb.	2 cts. per lb.
Paper	30 %	35 %
Silks	30 %	60 %

[1] On all forms of bar-iron, band-, hoop-, and boiler-iron, on chains, anchors, nails and spikes, pipes, etc., etc., the duties of 1864 were in force till 1883.

TABLE III.
Duties on Certain Articles, Raised since 1864 above the War Rates.

Articles.	Duty of 1861.	Duty of 1864.	Duty as Fixed in 1865-70.
Bichromate of potash	3c. lb.	3c. lb.	4c. lb. (1875)
Copper, ingot . .	2c. lb.	2½c. lb.	5c. lb.
Flax	$15 ton	$15 ton	$20 to $40 ton
Marble in slabs . .	30 %	5cc. cub. foot + 20 %	$1.25 to $1.50 cub. foot + 30 %
Nickel	Free	15 %	20c. to 30c. lb.
Steel rails	30 %	45 %	$28 ton
Umbrellas . . .	30 %	35 %	50 to 60 %
Wool	.3c. lb.	6c. lb.	10c. lb. + 11 %
Woollens :			
Carpets (Brussels)	40c. sq. yd.	70c. sq. yd.	44 to 70c. sq. yd. + 35 %
Cloths	12c. lb. + 25 %	24c. lb. + 40 %	50c. lb. + 35 %
Dress-goods . .	12c. lb. + 25 %	24c. lb. + 40 %	6c. sq. yd. + 35% 8c. sq. yd. + 40%
Flannels . . .	30 %	24c. lb. + 35 %	20 to 50c. lb. + 35 %

TABLE IV.
Revenue from Customs Duties, and Internal Revenue, 1861-1883.
(00,000 omitted.)

Year.	Internal Revenue.	Customs Revenue.
1861	None.	39.6
2	"	49.1
3	37.6	69.1
4	109.7	102.3
5	209.5	84.9
6	309.2	179.0
7	266.0	176.4
8	191.1	164.5
9	158.4	180.0
1870	184.9	194.5
1	143.1	206.3
2	130.6	216.4
3	113.7	188.1
4	102.4	163.1
5	110.0	157.2
6	116.7	148.1
7	118.6	131.0
8	110.6	130.2
9	113.6	137.2
1880	124.0	186.5
1	135.3	198.2
2	146.5	220.4
3	144.7	214.7

TABLE V.

Production, Imports, and Exports of Copper, and Foreign and Domestic Prices.

(Quantities in gross tons.)

Year.	Domestic Product'n.	Imports.		Exports.	Price per lb. in cents.		Difference in Price.
		Copper in Pigs.	Copper Ore.		New York Lake Cop'r.	London Chili Bars.	
1875	18,000	415	2,300	2,280	23	18	5
6	19,000	777	910	6,430	21.5	16.5	5
7	21,000	750	15	6,050	19	14.6	4.4
8	21,500	165	399	5,040	16.5	13.5	3
9	23,000	70	100	7,680	17.5	12.2	5.3
1880	27,000	2,350	2,000	1,880	20	13.5	6.5
1	32,000	320	4,420	2,160	18,5	13.3	5.2
2	41,000	334	8,190	1,490	18.7	14.4	4.3
3	52,000	148	500[1]	3,890	16.1	13.7	2.4
4	63,500	65	980	7,610	13.7	11.8	1.9
5	74,000	35	1,630	19,900	11	9.5	1.5
6	70,000	18	1,840	10,850	11	8.8	2.2

Figures are from "Mineral Resources of the United States," pp. 214, *et seq.* The production is for the calendar year, the imports and exports for the fiscal year (ending June 30th). The annual average prices are from the monthly prices given in "Mineral Resources." The figures given in "Mineral Resources" seem to contain considerable understatements, so far as exports are concerned. See *Eng. and Min. Journal*, Jan. 26, 1884, p. 59.

These tables show the price in New York to have been higher than that in London by from 1½ to 5½ cents. In recent years the great increase in domestic production

---

[1] Beginning with 1883, this column states the quantity of copper contained in imported ore, not the gross amount of ore. The 8,190 tons of ore imported in 1882 contained about 600 tons of copper.

has forced down the price here, and the difference in price is not more than 1½ cents. The better quality of domestic Lake copper would cause it to bring 1¼ cents more than Chili bars under any circumstances. Cost of transportation (from London to New York) is insignificant. It is safe to say that any difference in price over and above 1¼ cents per pound could not exist if it were not for the duty on copper.

TABLE VI.

Production, Imports, and Foreign and Domestic Prices of Bessemer Steel Rails.

Year.	Product in U. S.[1]	Imports into U. S.[1]	Average Price in U. S.[2]	Average Price in England.[2]	Average Difference in Price.
1871	38,300	not given	91.70	57.70	34.00
2	94,000	150,000	99.70	67.30	32.40
3	129,000	160,000	95.90	74.40	21.50
4	145,000	101,000	84.70	57.50	27.20
5	291,000	18,000	59.70	44.10	15.60
6	412,000	none	53.10	37.70	15.40
7	432,000	"	43.50	31.90	11.60
8	550,000	"	41.70	27.20	14.50
9	684,000	25,000	48.20	24.70	23.50
1880	954,000	158,000	67.50	36.00	31.50
1	1,330,000	249,000	61.10	31.20	29.90
2	1,438,000	182,000	48.50	30.00	18.50
3	1,286,000	38,200	37.75	25.40	12.35
4	1,119,000	3,000	30.75	22.90	7.85
5	1,079,000	2,400	28.50	23.65	4.85
6	1,769,000	46,500	34.50	20.65	13.85
7	2,295,000	154,000	37.10	20.65	16.45

The figures of production and importation are from the Reports of the American Iron and Steel Association, as are also those of prices in this country. The prices in

[1] In net tons of 2,000 lbs.   [2] Price per gross ton of 2,240 lbs.

England have been compiled from the files of the London "Economist," checked by occasional tables in the Iron and Steel Association Reports (*e. g.*, in "Report for 1879," p. 63). Prices by yearly average necessarily indicate only the general fluctuations ; but for purposes of general comparison the above are, I believe, trustworthy.

Cost of transportation varies from two to four dollars per ton. The difference in price over and above this sum represents the effect of the tariff tax. It will be noticed that in the years of activity (*e. g.*, in 1871–72, and in 1880–81) the difference in price is fully equal to the duty, which was \$28.00 per ton till 1883. In years of depression the difference in price is much less than the duty (*e. g.*, in 1875–78), and at such times importation ceases. In 1886, when the duty was \$17.00 per ton, the price in this country was higher than that in England by about \$14.00 ; under such circumstances, importation must evidently cease, the duty being prohibitory.

TABLE VII.

Changes of Duty in 1883.

Article.	Duty before 1883.	Duty Recommended by Tariff Comm.	Duty of Act of 1883.
Barley . .	15c. bushel	15c.	10c.
Copper, ingot .	5c. lb.	4c.	4c.
Cottons, coarse, .	5c. sq. yd.	3c.	2¼c.
" finer printed	5½ sq yd.and 20%	6c.	6c.
" mf. n. o. p. [1]	35 %	40 %	40 %
Files [2] . .	{ 6 to 10c. lb. and 30 %	35c. to $2.50 doz.	35c. to $2.50
Iron ore . .	20 %	50c. ton	75c.
" pig . .	$7.00 ton	$6.72	$6.72
" bar . .	1c. lb.	$\frac{9}{10}$c. lb.	$\frac{8}{10}$c.
Linens, finer .	40 %	35 %	35 %
Manufactures of iron, brass, lead, pewter, tin, etc. . .	35 %	45 %	45 %
Marble, block .	{ 50c. cub. ft. and 20 %	75c. cub. ft.	65c. cub. ft.
Nickel . .	20 to 30c. lb.	25c. lb.	15c. lb.
Quicksilver .	free	10 %	10 %
Rice, uncleaned .	2c. lb.	1¼c.	1½c.
Silks . . .	60 %	50 %	50 %
Steel, in ingots [3] .	2¼ to 3¼c. lb.	2 to 3¼c.	2 to 3¼c.
Wool, value under 32c.	10c. lb. and 11 %	10c.	10c.
Woollens, dress goods [4]	{ 6c. yd. and 35%	5c. and 35 %	5c. and 35 %
	8c. " " 40%	12c. and 40 %	9c. " 40 %
" cloths .	50c. lb. and 35 %	{ 30c. and 35 %	35c. and 35 %
		35c. " 40 %	35c. " 40 %
Flannels, blankets, etc. . .	{ 20 to 50c. lb. and 35 %	8 to 24c. and 35 %	10 to 24c. and 35 %

[1] Manufactures not otherwise provided for, embroideries, laces, trimmings, etc., see p. 237. [2] See p. 240. [3] See p. 239. [4] See p. 235.

INDEX.

267

Made in the USA
Las Vegas, NV
20 February 2022

44270044R00154